ARDUINO
PROGRAMMING
FOR BEGINNERS

Tips and Tricks for the Efficient
Use of Arduino Programming

ERIC SCHMIDT

Table of Contents

Introduction

Since its inception in 2005, Arduino has grown exponentially and spread its popularity from Italy, its country of origin, to the rest of the world. This book is designed to familiarize beginners with Arduino and educate them on everything it offers.

From the main terms to the functions Arduino has to offer, the book delves into the benefits of the Arduino programming language. The book will take you through a brief introduction to Arduino, its history, and all the tips and tricks you'll need to boost your Arduino knowledge from a beginner to a seasoned user.

Additionally, we'll introduce you to some basic concepts and all the different IDEs that can be used with Arduino for maximum efficiency when using the programming language. We thank you for choosing Arduino Programming for Beginners and hope you'll enjoy your journey through the fascinating world of Arduino programming!

Chapter 1

An Introduction to Arduino

With the technological advancements of the modern age, people are increasingly exposed to some form of hardware or software on a daily basis. Whether it be professionals, hobbyists, or even ordinary people, this exposure has led to a technological literacy higher than ever before.

A higher literacy naturally means people are more aware and take a keen interest in the technologies surrounding them. Arduino programming is one target of such an interest that has led to its exponential growth. Since its inception in 2005, Arduino has progressed in leaps and bounds and traversed the borders of its home country, Italy, to the rest of the globe.

Whether you're attracted to Arduino for its flexibility, or you've seen projects that result from Arduino technologies, your attraction to the technology is the result of such an interest. Whatever it may be, before you get around to utilizing Arduino efficiently, you should familiarize yourself with its history and the concept of its existence.

What Is Arduino?

A solid definition of Arduino might be challenging to grasp for some beginners; this is because the explanation is often riddled with technicalities such as "open-source," "environments," and "IDEs."

All technicalities aside, the simplest definition of Arduino, provided by its official platform, states that Arduino is simply an open-source platform/community with hardware and software that is easy to use and understand.

Being an "open-source" platform, Arduino can be taught and redistributed without violating any sort of copyright laws. In other words, the founders/creators of Arduino have allowed everyone to experiment with their hardware and software legally by not owning the rights to any of the ideas behind the foundation of the platform.

With its "easy-to-understand" nature, Arduino software and hardware can be understood and manipulated even by regular people with little research. The Arduino community mainly centers around creating packages for use in robots and other electronic gadgets.

The "hardware" used by the Arduino community is termed microcontrollers. These are essentially micro-computers intended for small tasks, unlike conventional computers such as laptops, tablets, or desktop PCs.

How Does Arduino work?

People who work with Arduino usually have a specific product in mind. According to their goals, they purchase appropriate hardware and upload codes into it using a powerful operating system such as Linux, Windows, or Macintosh OSX.

These codes are uploaded into the device using a cable and are essentially a set of instructions mapped out for the microcontroller to perform; this can vary from producing a beeping sound when exposed to light to making a random turn after sensing a presence ahead according to the type of microcontroller chosen.

Why Do People Use Arduino?

Arduino is quite a popular and approved platform mainly due to its flexibility and availability. Overall, it has quite an uncomplicated user experience, making it easy to use while retaining enough versatility to appeal to more advanced developers and engineers. While Arduino isn't the only microcontrollers platform out there, it does offer a few advantages which contribute to its popularity over the others:

- **Arduino microcontrollers are relatively inexpensive.**

In fact, a significant reason behind the inception of Arduino was to create an inexpensive and straightforward programmable device that could be used for projects in interactive art design by novices and professionals alike. Consequently, Arduino boards are pretty cheap compared to the microcontrollers offered by some other platforms. While the most affordable Arduino board can be brought unassembled, even the assembled versions don't go above $50 in cost.

- **Arduino is an open-source platform.**

The benefits of an open-source platform go without saying. It provides opportunities for newbies to gain experience by tweaking around with official software without worrying about legal issues. In contrast, seasoned veterans can use the overhaul of the existing software and hardware to come up with and publish their version of the Arduino platform.

- **Arduino is cross-platform**

The Arduino IDE works across platforms. In other words, it can work in Windows, Linux, and Macintosh OSX, a quality not many microcontroller boards have. Hence, Arduino software and hardware are as easily accessible to Apple and Linux (which itself is open-source) users as it is to Windows users.

What Type of People Use Arduino?

Arduino is used by a vast range of people, which can be attributed to its inexpensive and cross-platform properties. People use it for hands-on professional development and hobby projects alike. While the Arduino programming language is widely considered easy to understand, it is still rich and complex enough for a beginner to grow and mature his career. Furthermore, it also has enough flexibility and potential to catch the eyes of the most advanced users.

With all of these properties, Arduino users do not fall into specific categories. However, some examples of people who use Arduino include:

- **Teachers and students** alike. They were, after all, the original consumer base intended for the product. Educators primarily use Arduino to construct low-cost experiments designed to highlight physics or chemistry principles or to get started with building robots or coding in general.

- **Architects and designers** can build inexpensive and interactive prototypes or models of their work to use as a reference for their full-scale projects.

Almost anyone can use Arduino, and this is precisely the case. Amongst the Arduino community, you'll find people of all ages and professions to share concepts with and improve your understanding of the platform further.

What Are Some Arduino Terminologies to Get Used To?

If you're looking to improve your manipulation of the Arduino programming language as a beginner, you'll have to ensure you're familiar with all the core Arduino terminologies and their uses.

Arduino's In-Board Terminologies

Up to this point, you've familiarized yourself with the platform's core concepts, such as its open-source nature and the implementation of microcontrollers as hardware. However, that isn't all. While the term microcontrollers can be used interchangeably with Arduino hardware, microcontrollers aren't all the Arduino boards have to offer.

Most microcontrollers have *digital pins* which run along the edges of the board. These *"digital pins"* are used for *input* and *output* tasks. The *input* is what prompts the board to emit a response known as the *output*. For example, in a simple nightlight project, the *input* would be the lack of light in the room; without sufficient light, the light sensor would send a signal to the microcontroller, which would prompt it to close the circuit and activate the nightlight, the *output*.

There are also *"Analog in"* pins, which are quite often located opposite the digital pins. These pins register a varying input, for example, quantities such as temperature and pressure, which can fluctuate with time.

The board also has *5V and GND pins* which can connect an extra 5V power to the board; the board also has a *USB connector*, which is mainly used to upload your instructions but can alternatively be used as a power source too. The *USB connector* is the main port used to connect the cable between the board and the device your code is on.

Aside from that, there are the *power and pin LEDs*. As the name states, the power LED signals whether the board is receiving power or not; the LED lights up when it does, making *debugging* easier. The *pin LED* is often a specific pin on the board and is used for debugging.

Other LEDs, such as the *RX and TX LEDs*, light up whenever information transfer occurs; this is usually when you transfer your code from the primary device to the controller. Your code or instructions are commonly referred to as *sketches*, and these pins blink rapidly whenever such a transfer occurs.

Finally, there's the *microcontroller* itself. The *microcontroller* exists on every Arduino board, and you can think of it as the brain; it receives your *sketch* and acts according to the instructions you've written. It'd be safe to say that without the *microcontroller*, there'd be no way for any function across the board to take place.

How Can You Get Your Arduino Projects to Thrive?

Its open-source nature is the most prominent and most popular Arduino feature. IT is a great reason why many people, novices, and experts alike, are attracted by the community and the platform.

Not only can you access the open-source platform itself, but you can also access thousands of other projects and documentation made by other community users. Documentation doesn't just mean jotting things down; when accessing documentation made by other people in the community, you get to access all the tools and the resources to accomplish a project in the most efficient way possible. In simpler words, you're learning from the mistakes made by other people and skipping a large part of the "trial and error" process that most newbie coders go through.

Of course, you don't have to just benefit from the experiences of the community; you can give back too. Whether you're working on Arduino projects professionally or just as a hobby, you can help pass on your experiences to others by documenting your journey from start to finish.

As an Arduino beginner, the best documentation you can do is to write code that thoroughly explains itself. This can include intelligently naming functions and variables so they can be self-explanatory. When documenting your project, you should make sure other coders can tell what's going on just by looking at the code; well-named variables and functions can go a long way in accomplishing that.

When attempting large projects, some developers use automated documentation; when utilized efficiently, the documentation from such software doesn't lose out to manually written documentation.

The next part of making the most out of your Arduino project is ensuring your hardware is adequately documented. The best way to document your hardware is to maintain a good list with pictures and videos of all the hardware used in your project.

All of these aren't just a way for you to get the most out of your project; they're also a way for others to benefit from your experience. Likewise, you can benefit in a similar fashion by reading through other people's experiences and documentation.

You can also find a lot of already made circuit diagrams to benefit from or make some yourselves when attempting your project. You can also make your own circuit diagrams by using an application such as *Fritzing* or hand drawing a circuit diagram and scanning it into your computer.

Finally, you should learn how to use revision control programs. There are a lot of excellent revision control systems online which can be used for free. However, a far superior option is to use Git. Although Git is intended for large projects and corporations, the benefits to be harvested are immense once you get around to utilizing it individually, which can only be achieved once you learn the ropes of Git.

Another advantage of Git is that it can be used almost effortlessly with GitHub. GitHub is an immense source-code hosting service offering free unlimited private pools and public repositories. There are other options too, but while GitHub isn't the only source code hosting service, it is the best option due to its vast repositories and unlimited private pools.

After you finish your project, you can upload your documented source code using Git and all the other documentation you've compiled.

Chapter 2

Getting to Know
Your Arduino Hardware
•▪•▪•▪•▪•▪•▪•▪•▪•▪

W e've discussed the main components of an Arduino board already. However, not every Arduino board has the same features and specifications.

Like every other microcontroller platform, different Arduino boards are meant for different purposes. Previously, we discussed the main features of the Arduino UNO board, which beginner users are most used to working with. Aside from the UNO board, there is the Mega 25600 Model, the Arduino Ethernet board, and many more.

With that in mind, if you want to learn how to efficiently manipulate Arduino, knowing the ins and outs of its hardware and what each board has to offer is primary.

We'll take you through three different stages to optimize your Arduino manipulation. In the first stage, we've already introduced you to Arduino, and next, we'll take you through each of its hardware to get you used to their specifications and the areas they can be applicable in.

In the second stage, we'll introduce you to the software side of the spectrum. We'll take you through the most common methods of optimizing your code and most of the details of the Arduino programming language.

In the third stage, we'll show you how these two intertwine together. Keeping in mind that this is a beginner-level book, most of our knowledge will be directed toward individuals who have little to no prior knowledge of the platform.

Different Arduino Boards

At the time of its inception, Arduino brought a great change to the microcontroller market. It would be safe to say that the microcontroller scene at that time was in upheaval.

This disruption wasn't because the Arduino hardware or software itself brought a cutting-edge innovation never seen before in the market; it was simply due to the fact that with the inception of

Arduino, working with microcontrollers didn't seem far-fetched for the average user anymore.

Prior to 2005, associating yourself with microcontrollers meant paying a hefty price for the microcontroller boards themselves and the tools needed to program instructions into the board since these were seldom made publicly available at the time.

Furthermore, most of these development tools were often based on the assembly language, or worse yet, other propriety languages, which were very difficult to learn and not appealing to beginner or intermediate level users. With Arduino, however, everything changed.

Arduino, being an open hardware platform, not only provided the microcontroller circuits but also all the other circuitry and component at a relatively low price. Furthermore, the development tools were essentially free; the Arduino IDE could be accessed by users of any platform/operating system since it was based on the C language.

With the importance of Arduino hardware emphasized, let's move on to the boards offered by Arduino and their different specialties and features.

The Arduino UNO

The Arduino UNO board is perhaps the most widely recognized board by users on and off the platform alike. This is because the UNO board is a favorite of Arduino programmers just starting out since it's the most basic and packed of the lot.

The Arduino UNO board is also the cheapest Arduino board around, and its popularity is highly considered to have made the platform what it is today.

All Arduino microcontrollers are based on the ATMega series. The UNO board is a culmination and, as a result, a massive upgrade of the technologies used in two of its predecessors, the Duemilanove and the Diecimila models, none of which, unfortunately, enjoyed the success of its descendant.

We've already discussed the main components found in most Arduino boards in the previous chapter. Now that you're familiar with a majority of the Arduino terminologies, it'll be much easier for you to understand what we're referring to when we discuss each of these boards,

The UNO board has around 20 pins, six of these are *analog in* pins, and the others majorly serve as input/output ones. It has a working frequency of around 16 MHz, mainly due to the use of a ceramic resonator, and it also has a flash storage memory of around 32 KB.

The 32 KB memory is sufficient enough to execute most programs designed by beginner-level users and is sufficient enough for more advanced demands with minimal prototype specifications (which is usually for projects that are micro-controlled).

With UNO, you get a Type B USB connector port which makes connections convenient. Furthermore, the port can also be used to charge the board while simultaneously transferring data over from the main device.

Those aren't all the power options that the entry-level UNO offers; the main barrel plug works seamlessly with the standard 9v battery charger. The board has a nominal charging voltage between 7-12V; however, it operates smoothly even after small fluctuations, which makes its actual range more between 6-20 V.

The board is a great introductory specimen to get started with Arduino and is priced at around $25, with high availability at different shops and retailers due to its widespread popularity.

The Arduino Robot

Robotics is becoming increasingly popular throughout the world nowadays. As the name suggests, the Arduino Robot microcontroller is centered around controlling and manipulating robots.

As the worldwide interest in robots continues to increase, so does the development of microcontrollers. After all, stronger and more versatile microcontrollers allow more powerful and exciting robots to be built.

Robotics have a massive appeal, especially to the younger generation, who is heavily influenced by sci-fi movies and TV shows. Naturally, a manifestation of such interest means that a percentage of such people try searching for robots and how to build them.

For students and kids, such an interest in robotics means a perfect introduction to the chemistry of microcontrollers and programming, which would naturally lead to Arduino.

The Arduino Robot model is a totally operable robot, and it has a microcontroller similar to some of the other entries on this list. Aside from the robot model being designed with a robot in mind, there are very few differences in the core principles of what we've learned until now. For example, aside from the similar microcontroller, the programming language and the tools used to program it ultimately remain unaltered.

Hence, beginner Arduino users who want to transition over to the robot model will face little to no difficulties if they choose to do so. There are, of course, features specific to the Arduino Robot model, which makes it unique.

Aside from basic programming and manipulation, the Arduino Robot is unique in most of its functionalities. Unlike the other Arduino boards, the robot model is a combination of two different boards, namely, the motor and the control board. Both boards have their own features and are designed to carry out their own specific and entirely different tasks.

The Arduino Robot is equipped with LEDs (similar to other boards) and also has a compass, motors, motor drivers, wheels (all on the motor board), an IR sensor, wheels, speakers, and around five buttons situated inside the control board. It even has an LCD.

It has an ATmega32u4 microcontroller which, similar to the Arduino UNO, has around 32 KB of storage. Out of these, 32, 4 are allocated to the bootloader. Furthermore, it also has around 2.5 KBs of SRAM and a further 1 KB of EEPROM, which can even be read and overwritten accordingly, provided the right EEPROM library is used.

When it comes to power, the Arduino Robot is quite versatile; it can be charged using 4 AA batteries or by using the USB connection (just like the UNO variant). The robot's battery holder can hold 4 of these NiMh AA batteries at a time and should only be used with rechargeable batteries. Furthermore, all the motors associated with the Robot model are switched off when connected through the UDB to avoid any unexpected accidents.

Aside from that, it also has its main power supply, which requires a 9V external voltage which must be supplied through an AC-to-DC adapter. The motor board can be connected by taking any 2.5-mm center-positive plug already connected with an adapter and plugging it into the power jack.

A major difference, which is quite understandable given all the extra features it packs, is the price difference. The Arduino Robot Model is more expensive than the other Arduino boards on the market; even then, compared to its competitors, it falls on the cheap end of the spectrum.

At the end of the day, all you need to do to get started on Robotics with Arduino is to squeeze out a little more money than usual and opt for the Arduino Robot Model.

The Arduino Mega 2560

The Mega 2560 is Arduino's answer to people who need a more powerful board with a lot more functionality than the traditional

Duemilanove and the Diecimila. It is also longer than their descendant, the Arduino UNO, and also has a different footprint.

Just like its name implies, the Mega 2560 board has an ATmega2560 microcontroller which has a 16 MHz working frequency, just like the UNO. However, unlike the UNO variant, the powerful Mega 2560 has a much higher peripheral number.

Furthermore, the Mega 2560 comes in with the guns blazing when it comes to its memory/ storage. It offers a flash memory with a size eight times that of the UNO, around 256 KB to be precise. This makes the Mega 2560 more than capable of handling complex tasks and instructions.

While the Mega 2560 holds little to no allure for beginners, it is a board you'll inevitably have to use if you decide to further pursue programming with Arduino.

There are multiple reasons for the Mega 2560's popularity; one of these include its whopping 52 digital input/output pins; out of these, 15 can be used for *the analog output* (with the use of *Pulse Width Modulation* or *PWM* in short), and a further 15 are used for *analog input.*

Furthermore, the Mega model also has the four added sports for serial communication, and six hardware interrupts, each different coupled along with a communication SPI port.

Aside from that, the Mega 2560 remains pretty similar to the UNO model in other aspects. It has a similar power setup; it can either be charged through a USB port or the main power jack, which has the same range of input as the UNO model (from 7-12V ideally and between 6-20V under less-than-stellar conditions).

The Mega 2560 is the perfect choice for people who want to carry out complex tasks with more versatility than the UNO board can handle.

The Arduino Ethernet

The Arduino Ethernet board has an added Ethernet interface which makes it easy for you to connect the projects you develop directly to the internet or, alternatively, to an Ethernet network.

The Ethernet board was presented as an idea to represent IoT, the Internet of Things, and it accomplishes its purpose pretty successfully; however, there are a few tradeoffs.

The Ethernet board is quite similar to the UNO model. Since it has the same microcontroller, the ATmega328, the Ethernet board also has the same memory (around 32 KB) and all the other distinctive features of the UNO model.

However, since the board also has the Ethernet module, a lot of the features of the Ethernet board fall short of those of the UNO board.

For example, the number of input/output pins on both the UNO and the Ethernet model number around 14. On the Ethernet model, you can only use nine because the rest are reserved to be used in the interface for the Ethernet module.

Also, there's the USB port tradeoff. The Arduino Ethernet board does not have a USB port. Not only does this cut down on a potential power source (in case anything ever happens to the main method of charging the board), but it also removes a seamless and hassle-free method-of data transfer.

In place of the USB port, the ethernet board has a six-pin male connector which can be connected from the microcontroller to your device using a serial-to-USB converter. This converter is better known as an FTDI cable and is necessary for data transfer to take place between your primary device, which holds your sketch, and the microcontroller due to the FT232RQ chip on the cable.

The Ethernet board does, however, have its own advantages. Unlike some of the other boards, Arduino's Ethernet module comes with an integrated Micro SD card reader; this means that you can store files and a lot of resources exponentially bigger than what you were able to store on the UNO model. There is, however, a simple catch, to access the external SD card reader and to get to use it, you'll have to use an external library, and for that, you'll have to learn what external libraries are and how to use them.

Furthermore, while the board doesn't have a USB port to use as a charging method, other alternatives exist. Aside from using an FTDI cable to connect the six-pin male connector to a USB port and then to your device, you can directly use PoE (Power over Ethernet) module to get your device to charge.

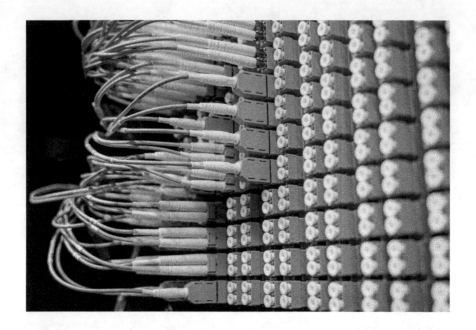

The PoE module allows your board to charge itself from its own Ethernet connection. Think of it as killing two birds with one stone; by using the PoE module, your board only has to be connected directly to the Ethernet, where the other tasks and the charging of your board take place simultaneously.

The PoE module cannot be bought as a shield or as an add-on to your Ether board. You'll have to order it alongside your board when you order it. And it really isn't that bad of a deal, considering it lets you kick back on a major issue with the original Ethernet board.

The Arduino Yún

Unlike some of the other boards on this list, the Yún board is a fairly recent addition to Arduino's roster of boards. While it also incorporates the concept of IoT like the Ethernet board, it does so slightly more uniquely.

Unlike the Ethernet board, the Arduino Yún has two different sections incorporated together. This is similar to the two entirely different boards interconnected on Arduino's Robot module.

Just like the Robot module, these two interconnected sections on the Yún board have an entirely different purpose and structure. One side of the Yún board is incorporated with the standard Arduino board. It has all the regular pins, LEDs, and most of the other devices and outlets we've grown familiar with. In the other section, the Yún board has a totally different and entirely operatable Linux device that has Ethernet and Wi-Fi support.

With such a setup, users stand to gain the best from both areas. You can take advantage of the flexibility provided by Arduino while also making use of all the freedom and connectivity options that come along with a Linux device. Furthermore, you can also use the Linux device to make small programs and shell scripts using an easy-going language such as Python.

Once you take a look at the specifications and the features that this board has to offer, you'll quickly realize the power the board holds to create projects imbued with the essence of IoT.

When talking of specs related to the Arduino side of the board, the microcontroller is an ATmega32u4 board (which, if you might remember, as mentioned in the Arduino Robot part of this section) that runs at around 16 MHz frequency and has around 20 digital input/output pins. Out of these 20 pins, around seven can be used as *analog out* pins (using *PWM,* as we already explained); the board also has 12 more pins used as analog pins.

When it comes to the Linux side of the spectrum, the board runs on an Atheros AR9331 chipset, which overshadows everything else we've studied up to here in terms of flash memory. The Atheros AR9331 chip has a flash memory of around 16 MB, which can, alternatively, also act as the device's hard drive. Out of this 16 MB, around nine is dedicated to handling the OpenWrt, which, in simpler terms, is the operating system inside the Linux part of the Yún board, and the chip also has a clock frequency of 400 MHz

Aside from that, the Yún board is the superior option compared to the Ethernet board simply because it delivers where the Ethernet board fails to do so. Like the Ethernet board, the Yún board also offers a Micro SD card slot for added storage and versatility. Furthermore, the Yún board still provides the added functionality of a USB connector.

It does fall a bit short when it comes to the power side of the spectrum. The Yún can only be charged through the USB port and does not have a voltage regulator. There are, however, ways to work around this, and while charging the board using an external battery pack may be difficult (due to the absence of a voltage regulator), it still isn't impossible.

All in all, the Yún is definitely an all-in-one package. It has the best of what Arduino boards have to offer, and along with its Linux compatibility, the board is perfect for not only developing your physical project immaculately but also connecting it to the network.

The Arduino Micro, Mini, and Nano

While these aren't individual boards, they're a very popular subfamily inside the major Arduino family. Arduino's Micro, Mini, and Nano boards are very popular amongst the general Arduino community.

While the name of these three boards might actually point towards the same thing, they're actually three different boards, each of varying length with similar features for the most part, which is partly the reason why they're being introduced together.

These boards are not much bigger than the standard postal stamp (with dimensions around 2 inches in height and 0.75 inches in width). Furthermore, they're also not much different in ability and characteristics than other members of their family. It's just that these boards are designed to be more compact and convenient to use, a feature their small size accomplishes quite easily.

With their dimensions, the Micro, Mini, and Nano boards are the perfect boards to connect directly in projects with a tight space and to the *breadboard* (more commonly known as the *plug block,* is mainly used to build circuits that are temporary in nature, they're widely used because breadboards allow components to be used, removed and replaced easily without any need for soldering).

If you want to pry into the technicalities of the matter, the Arduino Nano and Mini boards are equipped with an ATmega328 chip (the same used in the UNO) rather than an entire microcontroller. The Arduino Micro, on the other hand, is equipped with the ATmega32u4 microcontroller, which as you might remember is the same microcontroller used in the Arduino Yún and the Arduino Robot model. While there is a slight difference in the chipset, all three of these boards have a 16 MHz working frequency and are equipped with a flash memory of about KB, which is useful in storing and executing your sketches.

Now, on to the number of pins, the Nano and Mini board once again fall short of the Micro board since they both have around the same number of pins as the UNO board, only that they have a higher number of *analog* pins (around 8 in total). The Micro Board, on the other hand, has around 20 pins meant only for digital input/output means, out of which around seven can function as *analog output* pins due to using *PWM.* In total, the Micro board has around 32 pins since it has 12 more pins that are labeled as *analog input.*

When it comes to the power supply, the boards can vary. Starting with the Mini board, it doesn't really have any power supply options or facilities. This is because the board is as small as it is, it naturally falls upon you to design your project in a way that provides a regulated power supply for the board to run.

On the other hand, the Micro and the Nano boards are a bit easier to use. They both have an integrated USB port with micro and mini-USB connectors, which can be used to power the board and transfer data.

Furthermore, these two boards also have a serial port, unlike the Arduino Mini board, which means that both can be used to communicate with other boards that have serial capabilities.

At Arduino, all of these smaller boards were designed with only a single goal, to work directly on the core of the microcontroller and make it self-sufficient such that the body of the board could be reduced as much as possible. Smaller boards that do not lose out to the productivity levels of any of the larger boards while still saving tons of space for further maneuverability within the project are surely a big catch to have, don't you think so too?

Chapter 3

Setting Up Your Arduino Journey for Maximum Efficiency

Programming essentially refers to developing software applications. When programmed, software controls hardware, which generally refers to the part of an electronic gadget that is visible.

All hardware follows a programmed set of instructions that controls its actions. This includes complex electronic gadgets such as tablets, personal computers, laptops, and other devices. This written code is often referred to as the source code.

Introduction to Source Code and IDE

What Is Source Code?

In simpler terms, source code is a plain file containing code belonging to a specific programming language. Generally, source code files are correctly formatted, well-executed, and efficient. When using Arduino, source code files are often waved with a ".c" or a ".ino" file extension; for example, a text file named project1 with Arduino code would be saved as "project1.c" or "project1.ino".

You can write source code using any *full-screen editor*. While all full-screen editors will execute the same task at the end of the day, some editors offer a few features that rank them above others. Features such as *syntax monitoring, color coding*, and other tools can be pretty handy when writing long codes.

When executed, the source code transitions over and becomes the *object code*. This code is produced by a *compiler* that runs through the program when it is executed. The conventional compiler used in the compilation of Arduino code is known as *CC*, and it represents the C compiler; this is due to the fact that Arduino is closely based *on C/C++ and Java*; therefore, it has a similar compiler.

Source code files that have transitioned over to object code are saved with a ".o" file extension; as for their name, it is the same as the initial file name you set. Once the object file is created, the object code is connected to the Arduino language libraries in a process commonly referred to as *Linking*. These libraries are what make programming in the Arduino language worthwhile. They are full of functions and routines applicable to many gadgets and are actually the powerhouse behind making your code more efficient. We'll take a look at some Arduino language libraries later.

If the process is over smoothly, a final program file is created, which can be tested by running. If the program runs the way you want it to, it is deemed a success; otherwise, the entire process is repeated. All of the tools involved in these steps, for example, the *Linker* used in linking and the *compiler* used while compiling, originate from the command terminal. Alternatively, many seasoned programmers use the command prompt directly to capitalize on the faster execution time. Either that or you could just resort to using a fully-fledged Integrated Development Environment, which would have a lot more features with its own compiler, linker, and other command prompt tools.

What Is an IDE?

An IDE is a fully-fledged tool for source code development. It puts together all the tools required for editing, compiling, running, and connecting code in one place. Not only that, but it also goes beyond to include other mechanisms for debugging, has a variety of different functions which help to produce complex programs, and has visual tools.

Finally, it has its own command prompt compiler and Linker. While the overall process remains the same whether you use a simple text editor or an IDE, there is a tremendous difference in efficiency when comparing both. Of course, this difference is barely noticeable for people just beginning with Arduino; however, as you progress further, you'd rather have all the tools in one place with easy access rather than a simple text editor.

There are multiple IDEs on the internet. Users of the Macintosh OSX, commonly used in Apple devices, generally opt for the X code IDE, whereas Windows users generally tend to use Visual Studio as their IDE.

Arduino also has its own IDE; however, compared to some of the other IDEs we'll take you through, it lacks many features that seasoned programmers would prefer to have.

Best IDEs for Efficient Arduino Development

The Arduino IDE is a great development environment when it comes to beginners. It is a single-file-focused and straightforward development environment mainly created with novices in mind, and when all things considered, given its targeted demographic, the Arduino IDE does its job pretty well.

Since we're primarily focusing on beginners, we'll guide you through setting up the Arduino IDE since it is the best for complete beginners with no prior experience.

However, once you pass through the initial testing phase of the language and move on to developing real-time projects such as developing Arduino libraries and cores, the IDE simply doesn't do the trick anymore.

How to Set Up Arduino IDE

There are two options when it comes to using the Arduino IDE to manipulate your code:

1. You can download the desktop application of the IDE.

The desktop application has varying options to adapt to the type of device that you use. For instance, the Windows desktop application can also be accessed from a Windows phone or tablet; you don't need a Desktop PC or a laptop; however, your tablet or phone must have the Windows OS up and running.

The Macintosh OSX application can only be used on Apple Desktop and Laptops; there is no support for Apple iPads and iPhones.

Users of the Linux OS can choose between three different Arduino IDE options, the ARM, the 32-bit, and the 64-bit versions, according to their system configurations.

Finally, you can download the desktop application for your respective systems by following: https://www.arduino.cc/en/Main/Software

With that being said, once you've downloaded Arduino IDE, your file will most probably be in the ".zip" format. You'll have to unzip the file and set it up.

or

2. You can use the online IDE to code comfortably without the need to download anything.

Alternatively, you can also resort to using the online variant if you're not in the mood to download the IDE. However, the web application should only be used by individuals that not only have stable and fast internet connections (to prevent data loss) but also have no qualms with exceeding their data limits every once in a while.

Furthermore, the web application doesn't have any system requirements and can be used on all devices, including Android and Apple phones, because it has its own platform to run on.

Lastly, uploading your sketches to online web applications gives them an extra layer of security. After all, uploading your sketches to the web application directly uploads them to the Cloud, which is much more secure and can also be accessed using another device altogether, provided that you have the appropriate credentials.

At this point, you're probably wondering how your board comes into play when setting up your Arduino IDE. Well, we'll keep you waiting- NO LONGER!

How to Set Up Your Arduino IDE with Your Arduino Board

We've discussed the most prominent Arduino boards, and we've given you a glimpse of the types of Arduino IDEs you can work on as a beginner. While we'll be delving much deeper into all the different IDEs available to you later on, at this point, you should learn how these prominent boards and the Arduino IDE actually fit into a single picture.

- You'll have to start by purchasing your board. You'll find it much easier to establish a connection between both devices if your board, like the Arduino UNO and the Mega 2560, has a USB port for connection.

- With the Arduino IDE, you should continue from where we left off in the last sub-topic, unzipping your Arduino file (you can use WinRAR, a very popular unzipping tool, to achieve this).

- Once your IDE is unzipped, you should power up your board. Most Arduino boards, such as the UNO, the Mega 2560, and even the Duemilanove, draw power automatically from the USB cable without the need for any outside influence. Other boards like the Diecimila, however, have to be set up before they are able to draw power from the USB connection; this is usually done by making sure that the jumper (which is a small plastic that usually fits between two out of three pins) is fit right between the two pins that are situated the closes to the USB port.

- Once the link is established, your board's power LED should signal you with its signature light.

- After you unzip the Arduino file and establish a connection between your main device and the Arduino board, you'll have to launch the Arduino IDE application. Once unzipped, open the folder and search for an application with the infinity symbol icon (application.exe); once you find it, double click and start the Arduino IDE.

- Everything from this point on is pretty straightforward. After the Arduino IDE opens up, you can either elect an entirely new task or open an existing one. (You can create a brand-new task by clicking on File-> New or an existing project by *File->Example->Basics->Pre-existing Project Name*).

- After that, you have to select your Arduino board from within the IDE. You should always choose the name matching your board to avoid any sort of inconvenience. You can select your board by choosing Tools-> Board.

- Next, you'll have to select your Serial Port. Go to Tools-> Serial Port Menu to view all available serial ports. To find out your own serial port, disconnect and connect your Arduino board; the Serial Port Option that disappears and reappears is your Serial Port.

- After that, you can upload the program directly to your board by clicking on the horizontal arrow on the Arduino IDE.

After clicking on the upload, you'll see the TX and the RX LEDs flash, these LEDs signify the transfer of data taking place, in case you might have forgotten.

Tip To Remember: If you're using an Arduino Micro board or a similar variant, you'll have to reset the board before uploading your sketch so that the process occurs seamlessly without any error.

What Features Does the Arduino IDE Lack?

The Arduino IDE lacks some features, making it unattractive for more seasoned developers. These include:

An Integrated Terminal:

A considerable part of an IDE's allure is that it contains a standalone command prompt or terminal. Whether you use the Windows Command Prompt or, alternatively, Bash according to your preferences, there's no doubt about the importance of an integrated terminal.

Imagine changing windows every time you wanted to run a terminal command; while it may seem like a minor inconvenience at first, given the importance of the terminal in Arduino programming, missing an integrated terminal in an IDE just doesn't cut it.

Navigation Properties:

While navigation properties aren't needed in the beginner stages when you're writing 50 lines of code at maximum, it becomes increasingly vital as the scope of your projects continues to increase (which it naturally will since you're practicing a programming language). While it isn't much to find a particular line of code in a total of 50 lines, the same cannot be said for a code that is 500 lines long. Finding a specific code within large code bases can be quite a pain and, not to mention, time-consuming.

Most of the other IDEs, unlike Arduino IDE, offer many navigation features such as *find-by-reference* and *search-by-symbol,* which help locate a function's definition or symbols inside a file, respectively. Aside from that, quick navigation to errors within the source code file is also essential; finding an error directly instead of searching for it can save much time, especially when debugging.

Version Control:

Programming is primarily a process of trial and error, especially so for beginners; you never know when and where you might go wrong. This is where Version Control Integration comes into play. If you're adept at using the basics of Git, source control integration can show you every line that you've changed ever since you last commit using Git. This helps make changes more manageable, and knowing you already have a backup in place allows beginners to experiment with their code without worrying about losing their prior progress.

Refactoring and Auto-Completion:

Auto-completion works on a similar principle to suggestive texts in phones; based on the previously declared functions and variables, it helps to complete variable, constant, and function names. Furthermore, it also provides clues to the parameters required by a specific function.

What Are the Best Alternatives to Arduino Ide for Seamless Arduino Development?

The Arduino CLI

The Arduino community was thrilled when the platform announced its new Command Line Interface. After all, the use of the CLI allowed for effortless JSON file outputs which could easily be parsed by a wide range of other programs, a quality that made it very user-friendly across the whole developer community. However, the Arduino CLI is only recommended for programmers who love to use the command prompt/terminal.

While the terminal may be fast and minimalistic, there's a lot of maneuvering involved, especially in accessing the correct libraries for your project. When combined with the proper knowledge and a run-of-the-mill text editor, the Arduino CLI can just about compile and execute any program.

Once again, the CLI is only recommended for people with prior exposure to programming, and even then, only terminal enthusiasts tend to use the CLI.

Atom.io + PlatformIO

While Atom.io is only a text editor, it doesn't lose out to any IDE out there. When combined with an extension known as PlatformIO, atom.io becomes one of the best Arduino code editors, performing even better than IDEs in some aspects.

Contrary to standard IDEs, atom.io is quite fast, even with the PlatformIO plugin. The fusion between the two results in a code editor that is lightweight yet robust and extremely powerful when it comes to executing Arduino code.

While you'll have to learn how to create an *IoT* device with atom.io, the compiling process of the editor is seamless, and just like the Arduino IDE, it provides you with enough alternatives to choose your own board and port options. All in all, it is a well-rounded text editor that covers most of the Arduino editor's drawbacks with a highly intuitive design that takes little to no time to get used to.

Visual Studio and Visual Studio Code

The third option, and this time, a fully-fledged IDE, is Visual Studio. Visual Studio is fully compatible with the Arduino programming language; you have to install the Arduino add-on, and you'll be good to go and code.

Furthermore, while visual Studio might be a Microsoft IDE, it can also run cross-platform on Mac computers. You'll feel the advantages of a fully-fledged IDE when you take advantage of features such as Syntax highlighting, Serial debugs, error hints, and the ability to create charts. Also, most versions of Visual Studio aren't free; however, you can get a community developer license and code for free accordingly.

An excellent alternative to Visual Studio is visual studio code. While it isn't a fully-fledged IDE and is instead a text editor, you can use the appropriate plugins and extensions to make sure that it meets your taste. Finally, Visual Studio Code, unlike its IDE counterpart, is entirely free and is, in fact, one of the most popular text editors out there!

An Introduction to the Arduino IDE

Now that you've learned everything that there is to learn about setting up the Arduino IDE for yourself, it's about time you get to familiarize yourself with it. The Arduino IDE is fairly uncomplicated for individuals that have worked with the other development environments mentioned in this list. However, since this book is geared toward beginners, we'll take you on a tour of the IDE and take a look at all of the structures, parts, and tools that it offers.

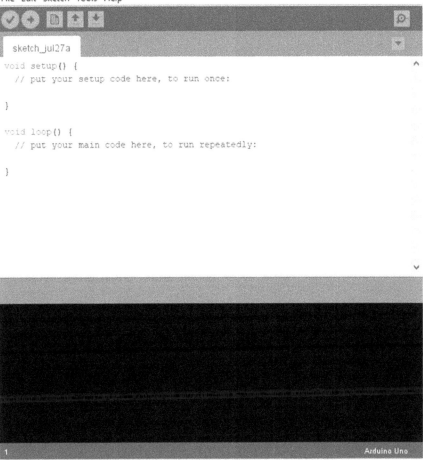

At first glance, you'll see that the Arduino IDE doesn't have much to offer in terms of the User Interface (UI). The Arduino IDE screen on the first run looks similar to this:

If you look at it close enough, you'll notice that the IDE is basically divided into four main areas:

1. The Main Menu: it has five menus, each of which contains its own commands.

41

2. The top toolbar is common in most IDEs and usually has the main tasks the IDE can perform. These buttons have common commands such as the upload button (the horizontal arrow) that we mentioned above.

3. Next, we have the code editor, which falls right in the middle after the top toolbar; this is where all the magic takes place; in other words, it is where you'll write your program.

4. Finally, you have the message area right at the bottom. The message area is vital, especially when it comes to debugging your program. The message area displays the current status of your sketch. It also pinpoints all possible locations in which errors have been found after the compiler has gone through the code.

Now that you have a basic idea of what each of these codes is used for, we can look at each in more detail so that you won't have to think much when using them in your sketches later on.

Arduino IDE Toolbar

The Arduino IDE toolbar has around six buttons used to accomplish six different tasks. These tasks are the most commonly used commands of the Arduino IDE and hence have been placed at the forefront in the form of buttons so that they can be easily executed. You can judge the other five commands by the one we've already discussed before, the button with a horizontal arrow or, in other words, the upload button. The upload button is used multiple times in almost every sketch; the other five buttons are almost at an equal level of importance, if not above; let's take a look at each and every one of them, including the upload button in more detail.

Starting from the left side of the order in the Arduino IDE (shown above), these buttons are meant to accomplish the following commands:

1. **The Verify Button:** Shaped like a tick, the verify button is used to verify the current code in your sketch. The verify button goes through each line of code that you write out and informs you if there are any errors within; if it finds no errors, the button verifies the syntax inside your sketch and compiles it too.

2. **The Upload Button:** We've already discussed the upload button in detail; however, let's take another look at it. The upload button, shaped like a horizontal arrow, is used to upload your sketch (which at that point is in the form of machine code) to the microcontroller you've connected. If your code hasn't already been compiled (and subsequently converted to machine code), the upload button prompts the compiler to compile the program, and if there aren't any errors, the resulting machine code is then uploaded to your microcontroller.

3. **The New Button:** The button is shaped like a page with a turned corner at its right end. There isn't much to the new button. As you might have already guessed, the new button

is used to open a new sketch whenever you're done working with your current one.

4. **The Open Button:** This button is shaped like a vertical arrow pointing upwards with a horizontal line at the bottom. When you press the open button, you'll receive a pop-up menu with all of your previously saved Arduino sketches. In short, the open button is used to open previously saved Arduino files within the IDE for further editing.

5. **The Save Button:** The save button is shaped like a vertical arrow pointing downwards with a horizontal line at its head. The button name itself is self-explanatory; it is used to save the current sketch (being edited inside the Arduino IDE) to your hard drive/disk.

6. **The Serial Monitor Button:** The Serial Monitor Button is shaped much like a magnifying glass with a few dots going through it horizontally, much like the search icon used in most search engines around the world. The Serial Monitor button is used to open the Serial Monitor Window; when opened, this window allows you to actually percept the exchange of data between your main device (this can be your laptop, desktop PC, or whatever you're on) and the Arduino microcontroller. We will learn a lot more about the Serial Monitor and serial communication in further chapters or, to be precise, in **Chapter 10: Serial Communication.**

And that's all from the top toolbar side of the spectrum. Now. Let's move on to the middle part of the Arduino IDE User Interface, that is, the code editor.

Arduino IDE Code Editor

The code editor is your workspace because almost everything you do (except for a few scarce things) will happen inside the code editor. As for the few scarce things that won't, you don't really need to worry about them at the beginner level.

With the code editor being where you'll spend most of your time, it is only natural that you take your fair share of time getting to know the place. You can open full-fledged projects with multiple files in the Arduino IDE. When you open more than one document at a time in the Arduino IDE or, in other words, if you open a multi-tab editor, you'll find a small new arrow pointing downwards and located at the right side of the tabs area. Once you press this arrow/arrow icon, you'll find an entirely different tab-related menu being opened to you, which will contain options like Rename or New, and it'll also help you to move from one tab to another (which can be quite a hassle if you have a very large number of files opened in the editor). Basically, the small arrow helps you in the basic manipulation of your files so that you won't need to minimize the Arduino IDE and locate the project folder and files unless you're doing something else entirely.

While the Arduino Code Editor definitely isn't the most powerful editor on the block, it certainly does get the job done. With the Arduino code editor, you get almost all the features you'll expect to find in a modern code editor (**Reminder:** Focus on the use of "almost all," not all in the sentence), which include features like the highlighting of syntax; in simple terms, syntax highlighting refers to how good code editors nowadays dye different parts of the code in different colors, for example, a variable might be dyed in a different color whereas a data type might have a different color entirely.

While you might misunderstand and think that syntax highlighting is there to make the code look prettier, that is simply not true. When code is dyed in different colors according to the criteria explained above, it becomes easy to declassify, read and understand syntax. With such color coding, you'll easily understand where a variable, constant, reserved word, or data type is.

Another great feature in Arduino IDE, which, once again, you'll be able to find in most modern IDEs, is how it highlights parenthesis on hovering. This is not similar to syntax highlighting; all parentheses are of the same color. What happens is that whenever you hover your mouse over the starting parenthesis of, let's say, a function, the Arduino IDE will highlight the ending parenthesis of the function, allowing you to clearly see where it ends. Being able to see the opening and the ending of such constructions means that you'll be able to identify a missing parenthesis quite easily if your program ends up with such an error.

Apart from that, there are also other useful features. For example, the Arduino IDE also has the Reference Search feature, which can help you out a lot, especially when you're exploring programs made by other people. Using the Reference Search feature, you can place your cursor on a word and search it directly in the ALRS (Arduino Language Reference Section), which is part of the Arduino website. The ALRS will then proceed to show you the help page of the specified word or function or the documents related to the specified word on the Arduino website. By using the Reference Search feature, you'll be able to get to know many functions, libraries, and terminologies used by other programmers, and hence you can improve your own knowledge, and subsequently, your code will continue to get better and better. (**Tip to Remember:** The Reference Search feature will only help you when you are faced with reserved words or functions native to Arduino or the Arduino community, the feature can't help you with things that are entirely up to the user's choice, for example, the name of a variable or function, etc.).

There are also other formatting commands you can use, along with some that help in documentation. You can view these commands by right-clicking on the code editor, which will present you with a pop-up menu that has most of these commands in place. Some examples of these commands include: comment/uncomment, which you can use to add a comment to an already existing line of code, or you can uncomment it. It is also helpful while documenting your code; other than that, there are styling options, for example, the Increase Indent and the Decrease Indent option.

Tip to Remember: A good piece of code will always have proper indentation and comments, not only do comments help you to remember what's going on in your code when you access it after an indefinite period of time, but it also helps others do the same, in case you ever share your code with others.

With that, we're through with the code editor area of the Arduino IDE, and we can move on to the final part of the Arduino IDE user interface.

Arduino Message Box/Area

The message area, as we discussed above, is the part of the Arduino IDE that will come in handy whenever you want to debug your program. Not only does the message area tell you the type of error your program has been faced with, but it'll also tell all the details of the error, where it has been found, and what else has obstructed it from carrying out the command that you have asked it to accomplish. For example, a pretty standard error for beginners is facing an issue whenever they try to upload their new sketch to their Arduino board. This can be caused by calling an undeclared function. The message area will not only highlight the line in which the error takes place, but it'll also display the following message:

> *Programname.ino: In function 'void setup()'*

> *Programname:lineno: error: 'functionname' was not declared in this scope*

You can substitute the name of your own program and the name of your own function in the *'programname.ino/programname'* and the *'functionname'* part, respectively.

When faced with errors, the Arduino IDE will always give its best effort to reference the error directly in your program and print out an appropriate message so you'll be able to fix it promptly. However, it is not always correct, which is why we said that the Arduino IDE will "always try its best."

While it isn't always located correctly, the fact that the program has an error is never wrong. A good course of action ins such a case is always to check two to three lines above and below the area where the IDE thinks the error is located. If you're familiar with programming in C, then you'll already know that such situations are common, and while it isn't really that common when it comes to Arduino, it's still better to know and check the surrounding code too instead of focusing on a line which may or may not have the error.

Arduino IDE Main Menu + Commands

We have discussed almost everything the Arduino IDE has to offer except the five menu options and the basic commands.

The menu options in Arduino are very similar to what you may have seen in many other applications (not necessarily limited to IDEs); these include very common ones such as the File, Edit, and Help options.

The file menu has a lot of basic commands such as opening a new sketch, opening a previously saved sketch, saving your sketch in the same or an entirely different file, and even just saving it. These commands within the file menu are also common to many other applications. However, you'll also find two additional options that might be new to you, for example: the *Sketchbook* and the *Examples* Folder.

The Sketchbook submenu has another submenu within it that contains all of your previously created sketches. This means you can easily access whatever sketch you deem fit within your Arduino IDE. It is, however, a bit of a hassle. After all, if you want to be able to access your sketches from the said folder, you'll have to place all your files within a specified folder where the Arduino DIE can fetch them if they're called upon from the aforementioned submenu.

When it comes to the *Examples* submenu, we've already discussed it in a previous topic, and further on, we'll also show you how to create your own examples if you want to!

Aside from that, we also have the Edit Menu, which has all commands directly related to editing, such as cut, copy, paste, redo, and the like, which are pretty common with other applications. When talking about outliers, you'll also have options such as "Copy as HTML" and "Copy for Forum," which can be used to publish the code (in the code editor) to a webpage. It can also prepare your code with all the proper formatting appropriate for a forum so that it can be published directly to the Arduino forum. The edit menu also has other commands mentioned before, specifically those used to clean the code up, for example, indentations and comments, and other commands to find words in code, much like other text editors.

Other than that, we also have the help menu, which has different commands that'll guide you to a different section of the documentation available on the Arduino platform. Also, you'll be able to view the frequently asked questions section on the website, which will give you a good insight into the problems faced by many people and their answers. For beginners, reading through the frequently asked questions section of the website will prove to be a great help as a majority of the questions and answers there are targeted at beginners that don't know their way around the IDE yet. However, although we doubt there'd be a need to visit the website given how much depth the book goes into, it still wouldn't hurt to check it out as you might end up learning something new!

Out of the total five options on the main menu, the three options which have a lot of common ground with other applications and IDEs have already been discussed. The two that are left are a lot more specific to Arduino itself; this includes the tools and the sketches option.

The Sketch option has many commands, some of which will be discussed in detail later. The most commonly used are the verify/compile option, the show sketch folder, which is used to open the project folder in which the disk sketch you're currently working on is placed, the add file option, and the import library option. Most of the names mentioned above are self-explanatory for the time being; as the book continues to progress, we'll discuss some of these commands in more detail, for example, the *import library* command.

Finally, we have the tools option on the main menu. The tools option has the Serial and Board port commands and many other options that will help you format your own code for a much easier time on the eyes while viewing.

Aside from that, the tools option also has some pretty convenient commands. For instance, the tools menu has a command that can create a ZIP package out of your project folder, allowing you to send and upload your file easily (be it via email or uploading to the cloud).

In the tools menu, you'll also be able to find the Serial Monitor command, which has pretty much the same function as its button counterpart on the top toolbar.

Fun Fact: You'll be able to find all of the commands on the top toolbar also present inside the menus of the main menu. However, they will all be divided between the five options in the main menu, which will make finding them a bit of a hassle. For instance, the verify/compile option (shown as a tick on the top toolbar) is also present in the sketch option on the main menu.

Chapter 4

Arduino Code Structure for Efficient Programming

We've briefly discussed the languages Arduino is closely associated with in the previous topics. Arduino code is based directly on C++ with the addition of a few extra functionalities and approaches. Since C++ is directly based on C, the Arduino programming language can be said to have been based on C/Java.

Like almost every other programming language, Arduino has a code structure in place that, when utilized correctly, can keep your code neat, clean, and efficient without any fluff. The structure's main elements responsible for this include functions, libraries, and classes/instances. We'll take a look at the most common aspects of the structure in this unit and move on to the usage and how they optimize code in the next.

Introduction to Arduino Code Structures

Libraries:

Like most programming languages, the Arduino programming language has built-in libraries that give basic functionalities for users to tinker around with according to their requirements. Of course, it is also possible to bring in other libraries if -the already existing ones don't satisfy your needs.

This is where the open-source quality of Arduino really shows itself. Instead of spending hours writing up code from scratch to perform a specific task, you can just search a library to see whether it already contains a function for the task you want to perform. Furthermore, since Arduino is an open-source platform, you have at least hundreds, if not thousands, of people sharing their codes with people in the community daily, making finding your code seem plausible.

We'll take an in-depth look at what libraries are, how to import them, and some of the best Arduino libraries.

Functions:

In Arduino, you can create your own functions and use pre-existing ones. Functions are simply pieces of code that can be used repeatedly in a program without having to write the entire code multiple times. Once a function is defined, you just have to call it to use it again.

Many beginners tend to make the mistake of copy-pasting a similar code instead of utilizing it as a function; not only does this make a program slower, but it also increases the unnecessary fluff and, consequently, increases the size of the source code.

Variables:

In simple terms, a variable is a storage location associated with a symbolic name; the value can be known or unknown. There are two main types of variables in Arduino; the scope of the variable determines these.

A variable may be declared and stored with a value, or it can also be used to store values obtained from sensors in Arduino boards. For a variable to be declared in Arduino, all you need to do is to define its name, type, and value (this is only the initial value, it can also act as a placeholder and be replaced later on).

Regional Variables

Regional variables are variables that are declared inside a block or a function. These variables can only be accessed by the code written inside the specific block or function that they are declared in. They are also known as Local variables and do not operate beyond the boundaries of their own blocks of code.

Global Variables

As you might have guessed already, such variables are usually defined beyond any block or function. Most programmers tend to declare global variables right at the top of the program. These variables hold their value and can be accessed throughout the program in which they've been declared. They can also be accessed by other functions declared later on in the same program.

Class and Instances:

In Arduino, the terms class and library can be used interchangeably. Simply speaking, a class is a collection of numerous variables and functions that can be used repeatedly to perform specific actions and tasks.

A class/library is similar to a function in that it lets you reuse a program without repeating the entire code; the only difference is that a class has multiple functions and variables that can be called numerous times throughout the source code.

On the other hand, an instance is the single occurrence/manifestation of a class. A single class can have multiple instances. For example, a class or an object named big cats might have multiple instances, such as a tiger, lion, and panther.

Loops

If you're familiar with programming to some extent, you'll already be familiar with what loops do; perhaps you might even have gotten an idea from the name itself. Loops do exactly what the name stands for: repeat a part of the program over and over until a certain condition is met.

Loops in Arduino are a piece of conditional code; these loops either run until a specific condition is met or until a specific condition is valid; it depends on the type of loop used. Loops are a perfect way to simplify and optimize your program and avoid cluttering.

Just imagine, without loops, you might have to repeat some instructions an unknown number of times, especially in some of the larger programs.

Chapter 5

Using Libraries to Optimize Arduino Programming

In the real world, libraries are great places to learn; they contain information about almost anything, and you'll find a lot of good stuff up there. Even nowadays, in the era of the internet, if you want to learn how to do something the old-fashioned way, you can find your way to the local library and find yourself the appropriate book, let's say, for example, "How to fix a motorcycle?" or "How to cook?". The point is, if you ever need to learn how to do something the old-fashioned way, you can run up to your old library, pick up a book, learn and return the book, all the while keeping your home uncluttered.

Libraries in programming work in a similar way. You can think of the home as your source code, and the library assumes its prior role in the scenario; however, instead of you taking the time out to actually read through the book, you just have to select the function (which takes the role of the book from the original scenario) and implement it.

In essence, a library is a huge collection of procedures, which are, in simple terms, instructions on how to do things. You can use the terms functions and procedures interchangeably.

Types of Arduino Libraries

The Arduino Programming Language has three types of libraries:

Standard Arduino Libraries

Standard libraries are essentially pre-existing Arduino libraries. These libraries are already included with the Arduino IDE when you download them. These libraries also include all of the examples that can be tested out as soon as the Arduino IDE is set up. We've already learned how to use some of these examples in the *"How to set up your Arduino IDE with your Arduino Board?"* section where we taught you how to use pre-existing projects.

These libraries are essentially the most basic of tasks and serve as an example to beginners in the language. They are also the most used commands, making common work a lot easier since they can be employed on the go.

Generally, Standard Libraries can be accessed in different ways, with the most commonly used method being to access the "Libraries" folder. If you happen to have different versions of the Arduino IDE installed on your primary device, each version will have its own variation of the Standard Library. These libraries also support the most common Arduino hardware, for example, LCDs.

Also, a tip to remember, try not to tinker around with your standard libraries; even when you learn how to install your own libraries, which we'll jump into in a while, you should try not to install your new libraries in the same folder as the standard ones.

Library Manager Arduino Libraries

The more recently released Arduino IDE version has granted users the ability to manipulate the Library Manager according to their wishes. The all-new Library Manager encourages the installment of libraries that have previously been submitted to Arduino for free use (Do you remember Arduino is open-source software? Anyone can contribute to the platform using their own versions of the code).

Using the Library Manager allows easy and convenient library manipulation; however, it can only be used in the most updated Arduino IDE versions.

User Installed Arduino Libraries

There are many other libraries to use aside from the Standard and Library Manager Libraries when it comes to the Arduino Programming language. In fact, these libraries don't even scratch the surface when it comes to all the other libraries filled with all sorts of useful functionalities for use. These libraries are available on a variety of third-party platforms; the most notable/renowned ones include GitHub, Google Code, and Arduino Playground.

Tip: Whenever you opt for a user-installed library, you should make sure that they are placed inside the Sketchbook libraries folder. In this way, you'll keep all your favorite libraries together in one place and won't lose any even if another major update for the Arduino library comes along.

Using the Library Manager to Install Libraries

Now, you already know how to use Arduino's Standard Libraries, so we won't pay much attention to that and instead skip over to the second library type, Library Manager Arduino Libraries.

Since the Library Manager is a relatively new feature, it has had the opportunity to integrate many useful libraries from the past to add to its collection. That fact, coupled with its ease of use, has made the library manager libraries a hot topic amongst Arduino users.

If you want to use a library that isn't included in the standard ones provided by Arduino, a good course of action would be to first check them up with the Library Manager rather than installing and integrating a copy of the library directly by yourself.

To do so, you'll have to access your Arduino IDE first. Once your IDE is flared up, you can select the *Sketch* option from the top menu (it will probably be the third option on the strip right alongside the *Edit* option and just before the *Tools* option) and then choose *Include Library -> Manage Libraries.*

After you've clicked on *Manage Libraries,* you'll be presented with a list of libraries that are available for you to install. Most of these libraries have been made by other users of the community who have made them available for use by others.

Arduino reciprocated the gesture by making them widely available by introducing the new Library Manager in their most recent IDE version. Another reason was that a large part of the community commonly used these libraries even before using the manager. While they weren't as common as the standard libraries included with the IDE, they were used enough to prompt Arduino to introduce their Library Manager feature to make access to such libraries easier.

Aside from the list shown, you can also use the search box to find any other library if you already happen to have one in mind. Often, many libraries are grouped according to the name of their producer; let's take Adafruit as an example. Adafruit is an open-source hardware company that also dabbles a lot in Arduino; consequently, they've also produced their own libraries, all of which are accessible using the Library Manager. You can search Adafruit using the search box on the Library Manager, and you'll be provided with a list of all the libraries that originate from Adafruit.

Now, once you've found the library you want, you can either install the library or, if it is already installed, you can choose the version of the library that you want. Oftentimes, in Arduino, the newest version isn't exactly the best option to choose; after all, the newest version isn't always compatible with older programs and can cause a few issues.

Sometimes, adding a library can also give you additional options to exercise in the *Examples* section under the *Files* tab (we've already learned about *Examples* and how to use them previously).

With the latest Arduino IDE versions, you get notified about all the updates available for the libraries that are currently in your use. You can ignore these notifications if you're working on an older project since the Arduino IDE doesn't update the libraries automatically. However, whenever you start on a brand-new project, you should remember to opt for the latest libraries as these are often much more efficient and value-packed than their previous versions.

Installing Arduino Libraries by Yourself

If possible, you really shouldn't resort to installing libraries manually; this is because the Library Manager is not only the easiest method of acquiring libraries, but it is also the safest.

The libraries available through the Library Manager seldom carry risks and are thoroughly screened and checked before being made available on the platform. User-installed libraries, on the other hand, do not carry the same level of security, and it is entirely up to your judgment to determine the associated risks.

However, sometimes, there simply isn't another option. Despite being sufficient for entry-level programmers, the Arduino Library Manager simply does not have an unlimited number of libraries. When it comes to some of the more complex tasks, it is only natural that the Library Manager might not have the perfect library available to make your work a lot easier.

To install a custom library, you'll have to manually download and place it into the library folder on your own machine. First, we'll skim through all you need to install a library on your local machine. After that, we'll go through the exact steps needed to install a library on each of the three different operating systems that Arduino is commonly used on (namely Windows, Macintosh OSX and Linux); to install a Library, you'll have to:

- **Create the correct folder manually.**

Arduino libraries have to be installed in the correct folder; otherwise, they won't really chime in when your program is running. If your files are stored in another location than what the IDE requires, the compiler will be unable to locate them during compilation. This can result in errors wherever you've tried to call upon functions from the library, and your sketches will not be uploaded to your board.

That isn't all; incorrectly installed libraries can also cause a lot of other IDE-related problems.

The correct hierarchy for storing libraries is:

Documents -> My Documents -> Arduino -> Libraries

In the *Libraries* folder, you should install the folder of whatever library you prefer, and your compiler will be able to access it whenever you execute your program. Arduino has a *Sketchbook* folder that stores all of the sketches you create within the IDE (whether they are uploaded or just simple sketches currently in progress); this folder is created automatically by the Arduino IDE itself when it's installed.

If you're using a device with the Linux OS, the folder name is straightforward: *Sketchbook.* In Linux, instead of the *Documents* folder, the *Sketchbook* folder can be found within */home/*.

On the other hand, the devices running the Macintosh or the Windows OS have a folder named *Arduino* instead of the *Sketchbook* name in Linux. You should remember that your libraries are not saved directly within the *Sketchbook or the Arduino* folder; rather, they are saved within another folder within the *Sketchbook* or *the Arduino* folder. Typically, this folder is named *Libraries,* and it is where the Arduino IDE redirects the compiler to look for the libraries mentioned within your sketch.

The more recent Arduino versions have simplified the process of downloading libraries manually. From Arduino 1.0.2 and later on, you'll find the *libraries* folder already present within your respective *Sketchbook* or *Arduino* folder; this is because the folder is created automatically by the IDE upon installation.

In earlier versions, you'll have to create the folder yourself whenever you try to install a new library. It isn't that hard; you just have to pay special attention to creating your library's folder in the right location to allow your compiler to easily access your libraries whenever you execute your program.

- **Use the Arduino IDE to create your folder.**

Alternatively, if you don't really want to create the folder manually, you can do it through the IDE. All you have to do is:

1. Open your Arduino IDE and locate the *File* tab.

2. Click on the *File* tab and look for *Preferences* from all the available options.

3. After clicking on *Preferences,* a new window will open; click on the *Browse* option present right next to the search bar.

4. Clicking on the *Browse* option will open the *File Explorer,* although, depending on your operating system, it might be called another name. Using explorer locates your respective sketchbook folder (as mentioned before, the folder might be called *Sketchbook* or *Arduino* depending on your operating system).

5. Once you've located your folder, select the *Libraries* folder if it is already created, and if not, create a new folder (by right-clicking *New -> Folder)* and rename it to *Libraries.*

6. Once you've renamed your folder, you're basically done with setting up your IDE to utilize user-installed libraries.

Installing Libraries Manually on Windows, Macintosh OSX, or Linux

Now that you're through with setting up your IDE to utilize your libraries, you have to learn how to install them. Typically, installing libraries is an easy feat; all you have to do is make sure that you're installing the correct library.

Due to the popularity of the Arduino platform, it has a vast community. It would be naïve to assume that everyone within the community who contributes to the platform is full of pure intentions or is relatively harmless (make no mistake, this is the case for most users). Therefore, you have to be careful whenever it comes to installing libraries or anything for that matter from third-party sources. To install a library manually on a device running with the Windows OS, you'll have to,

- **Shut down the Arduino IDE**

Before installation or anything else, you have to make sure that your Arduino IDE is closed. You'll have to check for all IDE's running instances to ensure it's not running. After all, the Arduino IDE only checks/scans for libraries within the folder at startup. In simpler terms, if your Arduino IDE is still running, even if you perform all the steps correctly, your IDE will not detect your library until the next initialization.

- **Secure Your ZIP file**

Once all running instances of your IDE are closed, you just have to download the file associated with your IDE. Typically, Arduino libraries that are made available online are compressed ZIP files; these files have a ".zip" extension and can be decompressed using a tool such as WinRAR.

Before choosing your library, aside from the credibility of the source (where the library originates from, you can usually find out a lot about a library from its documentation or even discussions of forums dedicated solely to Arduino development)., you should also pay a little attention to its status.

If you're choosing a library for development, the best you can do is choose a released version. The released version is meant solely for use, it has been tested and finalized by the creators of the library, and while there might be a few updates to the library in the near future (if the creators do continue to develop), there won't be many problems with the pre-existing code within the library.

The main reason why we're telling you to check for a released version is that Arduino is still an immensely popular platform. In simpler terms, people are still developing and adding their own code or, in this case, full-fledged libraries to the platform; some of the libraries you might opt for without checking might still be in their development phase, which means that they'll have untested, unreleased and buggy codes within which can render the library useless for you.

If you're downloading a library using GitHub, you can click on the *Releases* tab, which will guide you to all the released versions of the library that you're opting for; from these, you'll be able to choose from multiple versions of the library. As we mentioned before, if you're starting an entirely new project, you should opt for the latest release. Otherwise, you should opt for the version that your project is most compatible with.

Aside from that, you'll also be able to find the number of *commits* and the *contributors* to the library, which will tell you how regularly the library is updated and how large of a scale it really is on. Regularly updated libraries are also deemed more trustworthy and are better to have as they regularly bring new features and improvements.

- **Integrate the library**

Once you've unzipped your file, you'll be presented with your library master folder (which contains all of the library files) or the files directly, depending on what you chose while unzipping.

If you're directly presented with the files, you'll have to move them all to a single folder before proceeding. After that, you just have to copy and paste the master folder into the *"Libraries"* folder that you learned to create in the last sub-topic (**Reminder:** This is the *Libraries* that you may have created/found within your *Sketchbook/Arduino* folder).

After you've copied and pasted your library folder, you should ensure that it follows proper naming conventions. You should know that the Arduino IDE refuses to acknowledge/recognize any folders that have a dash in their name (underscores are not a problem!). Therefore, you must read through your folder name as it isn't uncommon for a GitHub file to have one or two dashes included within the name.

Finally, you've done nearly everything, and if you've followed our steps to a T, you'll be able to use call upon and use your library. After integrating your library, you should restart/start your Arduino IDE and check whether you are able to call upon the library and its functions seamlessly. If you aren't able to, that is, your compilation results in an error related to your library, check whether you've chosen the right folder and followed all of our steps perfectly.

What Are Some Common Issues with Installing a Library?

It is easy to slip up when doing a task that requires steps to be followed in a specific order, especially if you're relatively new to performing the said task; this remains true for installing libraries too. There are many common issues (mainly faced by beginners) when installing a library; in this section, we're going to discuss some of them. If you've installed your library and it seems to work perfectly fine, you can go ahead and skip this section. However, if your library isn't working, read on and don't feel bad, you're a beginner, and it is completely normal to make mistakes, this is exactly what this book is for!

- *"Library Name" does not name a type.*

The "Library Name" does not name a type, perhaps the most common error newbies face after installing a library. In simple terms, the does not name a type means that the Arduino IDE compiler could simply not find the library during compilation and hence cannot execute any of the functions or instances related to the library that you may have called upon in the program.

This error can have multiple reasons (some of which we have discussed before), which include:

1. Incorrect library name

2. Library Dependency

3. An incorrect folder location

4. Incorrect folder name

5. You might have forgotten to shut down all running instances of the Arduino IDE.

6. A partially or uninstalled library

7. Core Libraries

8. Missing Sketchbook Folder

9. Duplicate Libraries

You can have a look at each of these problems and their corresponding solutions below.

1. Incorrect Library Name

The name of the library you've mentioned in the *#include* section of your program or sketch must exactly match the name of the class in your library; this must be done word by word; in fact, you've to look out for even small details such as capitalization.

If the name of the class mentioned in your sketch and the name of the class in the library do not match each other, the Arduino IDE will not be able to identify the class, and hence, you will be faced with the "XYZ" does not name a type error.

Once you've integrated your library, you will be able to find example sketches related to the library in the same place that the examples related to the standard library are (**Reminder:** These examples are placed in *File->Example*). These examples already have the correct name of the class since they're loaded automatically from the library folder; therefore, you should just copy your class name directly from the example tab to avoid any inconvenience.

2. Library Dependency

Some libraries in Arduino are incapable of functioning alone. In simpler terms, in order for you to use said libraries, you'll have to download another partner library which will allow the main library to display its functions/features properly.

Let's take the example of some libraries belonging to Adafruit. We've already taken a look at Adafruit before; if you happen to install the Graphic Display Library belonging to Adafruit, you'll also have to install the GFX library of the same company. This is because the way the Graphic Display Library has been coded depends on some of the other libraries present in the GFX library to show its full potential.

Of course, this doesn't mean all of the functions and features of the dependent libraries are unusable. If we take Adafruit's Graphics Display Library once again as an example, you'll be able to use most of the features of the library. The only ones that'll result in the "XYZ does not name a type" error are the parts of the library that are dependent on the GFX library.

3. Incorrect Folder Location

We've already discussed this point before. The Arduino IDE compiler only refers to the *Sketchbook* folder whenever it compiles a sketch. You'll probably get an error if your library is not in the said folder or its Windows/Macintosh counterpart.

Furthermore, your main library folder must be directly within the *libraries* folder. If your main library folder is within another folder that is within the *libraries* folder (in other words, if the main library folder is a subfolder of another folder within the *libraries* folder), the Arduino IDE will be unable to access the library, and you'll get the corresponding error.

You should know that some library repositories (sourced from GithubGitHub) sometimes have entirely different folder structures. For example, the actual library folder might be two or three folders deep within the top-most folder. In such a case, as we stated above, you should rearrange all the folders and files to make sure that the library folder is the top-most subfolder within the *libraries* folder.

We've already discussed how you can deal with errors related to an incorrect folder location. In fact, if you're faced with the "XYZ does not name a type error," the first troubleshooting step you should take is to verify whether your library is installed within the correct folder.

4. Incorrect Folder Name

You shouldn't forget that the Arduino IDE doesn't really acknowledge libraries that have certain characters in their name. Unfortunately, these special characters happen to include the dashes "-" generated automatically by GitHub during installation.

Whenever you integrate a library, be sure to check the library name and just replace any dashes with underscores to avoid further errors.

5. Forgetting to Shut Down Arduino IDE

Once again, we've already discussed this, but let's give you a recap. The Arduino IDE scans for libraries only when it starts up. This means that if you want your newly installed library to work seamlessly with your code, you'll have to restart the Arduino IDE entirely. Alternatively, you'll have to make sure that all instances of Arduino IDE are closed before you begin your installation process.

6. Partially Installed or Uninstalled Library

You might have left your library partially installed in a hurry. Partially installed libraries cannot function and often result in errors that leave the whole program unusable.

Thankfully, it's quite easy to deal with partially uninstalled libraries. You can just reinstall the entire library. Furthermore, you can also cause your library to be incomplete if you tamper with any of the files that are present inside the library folder.

To help with your understanding, you can think of a library as an intricately woven web where each of the strings is reliant upon each other; breaking one string can cause the other to weaken and break, and consequently, the whole web collapses.

In a library, each of the internal components, in one way or the other, are reliant upon one another. If you, as a beginner, tamper with the files inside of the library, for example, you omit or change the name of any file, your entire library might just become unusable. You would have to reverse your changes or reinstall/unzip the library folder again.

7. Core Libraries

Some libraries are special. You can think of them as the numerous "classified" places throughout the world. These libraries cannot be used directly just by downloading.

Similar to said classified places, you must fulfill certain conditions before you can use these libraries. A prime example of a core library is Adafruit's GFX library, which itself is classified as a core library. For you to use the GFX library, you have to have a specific driver library compatible with the GFX library and the specific display for the task.

The mechanisms of core libraries are somewhat similar to the library dependencies we mentioned above. You can even think of it as a somewhat different type of library dependency, except that the requirements of core libraries aren't always limited to downloading other libraries; sometimes, they need a specific piece of hardware too.

8. Missing Sketchbook Folder

Sometimes, you might not have a folder labeled *Sketchbook* or *Arduino,* the name of the folder created can vary wildly depending on the version of the Arduino IDE you've installed or even the version of the operating system.

Of course, the folder isn't missing, only that the name has changed. Typically, the name does not change; however, sometimes, you just might not find a folder with a name similar to what we've discussed until now. In such a scenario, the best course of action is to open up your Arduino IDE's documentation and click on the link labeled "Where to Install your Libraries," which will guide you accordingly to the folder you must find on your specific device.

9. Duplicate Libraries

Duplicate libraries can mean two things. You have downloaded the same library twice, both of the same version, or you have two different versions of the same library.

When two copies of the same library exist in the *libraries* folder, the Arduino IDE tries to load each and every one of them. When it does so, it results in compilation errors within the program. Furthermore, it isn't enough to simply change the names of both folders; even if you name both of the libraries completely different, compilation errors will still arise.

If you cannot afford to delete one version of the library, i.e., you have two equally important programs, one of which might run the previous version and one of which might run the newer version, there is a solution. Whenever you require one library to run your program, for instance, you require the previous version of the library to run a program, you just move the newer version of the library out of the *Sketchbook* folder so that the folder remains out of the reach of the Arduino IDE.

How to Create Your Own Libraries

With everything about libraries said and done, the next step is naturally learning how to create your own library, whether you do it for your own use in the future or for you to publish/commit it to GitHub.

Since this is a beginner-level book, we'll only be showing you how to create simple libraries; after all, creating your own simple libraries can go a long way in helping you to optimize your code. Not only that, even if you start committing your library to GitHub as you learn to grow more proficient in Arduino, this will give you a much more professional take than others on the same level as you.

Step 1: Writing a Program

We'll get you started with the basics of creating your own library. Before you set around to giving your code the face of a library, you'll have to start from the bottom and create a basic program that will later evolve into a fully-fledged library.

We'll get you started with a very basic program that sums up two integers taken as input; in this program, we'll also demonstrate examples of a function for you!

```
1  int sum(int x, int y)
2 ▾ {
3      return x + y;
4  }
5  void setup()
6 ▾ {
7      Serial.begin(9600);
8      int result = sum(4,3);
9      Serial.println(result);
0  }
1  void loop() {}
```

This program was written using the online Arduino Editor. The int sum() {}, starting from line 4 and ending at line 5, is a whole function; this function is then later called on in line 8. Furthermore, the void setup() {} and the void loop () {} are also functions. Although they are automatically included as part of the program by the IDE, we'll be taking a deeper look into them later on.

As you might have already guessed, functions are denoted by the parenthesis "()" included with their name. Also, if you're wondering about the Serial.begin(9600) on line 7, just know that it is also a function. Rather, it is a function that passes the 9600 value within the parenthesis to the speed parameter, which essentially tells Arduino to exchange data/messages at a rate of 9600 bits per second with the serial monitor.

At this point, the code is all part of a single file; now, this might be ideal for a short program such as the one written above, creating a library with the same standards (that is, having all of the code in one file) isn't exactly practical. To create a library from this code, you'll have to separate the main code in the program from the rest of the code.

Step 2: Separating the Main Code from the Rest of the Code

To create a library, you need at least two files (yes, that's practically all you need to define your code as a library); one is the header file, these files have a ".h" extension, and the other file is known as the source file (**Reminder:** refer to the meaning of source code in the previous topics to get a better understanding of what source code actually means), these files have a ".cpp" extension.

The header file is simply a summary of everything the library offers, whereas the source file is where all of the source code is kept/programmed.

Now, to locate your own sketch, you can head to the *Sketch* option on the top menu bar and then the *Show Sketch Folder* option; this will then lead you to the location on your device where your sketch is located.

In your program folder, you'll already have a ".ino" Arduino file, which would have whatever name you set when you saved the program; let's take the name "program1" as an example. If you went along with the name we set, your program file would be named "program1.ino" and would be located inside a folder named program1.

Within the program1 folder, create two new files right beside the program1.ino file, with the names of "ownlibrary.h" and "ownlibrary.cpp" these are the header and the source files, respectively. Afterward, restart your Arduino IDE so that it opens the rest of the two files along with your main file after refreshing.

Now, you'll have to write a small piece of code in each of the three files.

The ownlibrary.h file:

```
1   #ifndef OWNLIBRARY_H
2   #define OWNLIBRARY_H
3   #include <Arduino.h>
4   int sum(int x, int y);
5   #endif
```

In the ownlibrary.h file, write the following code. The #include statement on line 3 is a must to include in the header file. This is because this include statement gives the file access to all the constants and standard types of the Arduino language, while this feature is added automatically to normal sketch files (or in other words the files that have a .ino extension), in library files, you have to add them yourself.

Furthermore, the #ifndef on line 1, the #define on line 2, and the #endif on line 5 is a whole construct to wrap around your header, and it is fail-safe to keep your library/their program working even if someone *#include*'s your library twice in their program.

Also, it is a good practice to write the name of your file in Uppercase, as demonstrated on lines 1 and 2, and to include an "_H" at the end for the name of the header guard; it makes your header file seem professional.

Finally, you should also include a comment at the top of your header, which should include its name, the name of the creator, the date of creation, the date of the last update, and the license; while these aren't exactly compulsory, after all, comments don't really alter the working of an Arduino program in any way, to remind yourself of the importance of such documentation and why you should get yourself used to it from the initial part of your journey as a programmer (whether it be Arduino or programming in general) refer to the "How can you get your Arduino Projects to Thrive?" section of the book.

If you already haven't noticed, we've already demonstrated how the header file is simply a summary of the source code. While we haven't filled the source file yet, you already know what'll be included as the source code since we've already demonstrated the initial file (which was to split into two).

The ownlibrary.cpp file:

In the source code file, or in other words, in the ownlibrary.cpp file, you don't really have to do much (remember, this is only because the source code for the function we've chosen is close to negligible, if we consider a program implemented on a large scale or on a full-fledged project, the source file would probably be one of the heaviest out of the lot).

All you have to do in your source file is:

1. Import/Mention your header file.

2. Write down the code for the function.

Once you're through with that, your source file should look something like this:

```
1   #include "ownlibrary.h"
2   int sum(int x, int y)
3 ▾ {
4       return x + y;
5   }
```

Now you just have to use the *sum* function in your initial sketch again.

The program1.ino file

Just like the source file, you'll have to include the header. Besides that, the sketch file remains relatively unchanged except that you'll have to remove the *sum* function since it has already been included in the source file. After all the changes, your sketch file should look something like this:

```
1   #include "ownlibrary.h"
2   void setup()
3 ▾ {
4       Serial.begin(9600);
5       int result = sum(4,3);
6       Serial.println(result);
7   }
8   void loop() {}
```

Now, since we've separated our code properly, we can finally give our code the shape of a library!

Step 3: Shaping Your Library

After separating your code properly, you can finally start treating it like a real library. At this point, you should already know that the Arduino libraries are placed within a specific folder; otherwise, the compiler cannot access them. Now it is time for you to place your own libraries within the same folder.

First, however, you'll have to move your source and header files into a single folder. Move your .h and .cpp file into a folder with the same name; if we were to continue the same example from before, you'd have to name the folder ownlibrary. Once the ownlibrary.h and the ownlibrary.cpp file has been moved to the ownlibrary folder; you've finally found your main library folder

Just like we did during the "installing a custom library" section of the book, we'll have to copy/cut and paste the ownlibrary folder into the *libraries* folder within the *Sketchbook or Arduino* folder (depending on whether your device runs Linux or Windows/Macintosh OS). After that, restart your Arduino IDE since it only scans for libraries on its launch.

Once again, in your program folder, you'll only have a single sketch file remaining in the main program1.ino file, you'll have to change the first header line a bit, you'll have to convert the "" to <>, like this:

```
1  #include <ownlibrary.h>
2  void setup()
3 ▾ {
4    Serial.begin(9600);
5    int result = sum(4,3);
6    Serial.println(result);
7  }
8  void loop() {}
```

You'll only have to do this in the sketch file for a simple reason, whenever you use a header file located within the same directory, for example, previously, all three files were within the same folder; hence their directory was the same and "" were used. Now, however, only the header and the source file remain within the same directory, hence why the source file still uses the "". On the other hand, if the header file is installed globally, which is the case since the ownlibrary folder is now treated as a full-fledged library and is no longer located within the same directory as the project directory, the sketch file or the program1.ino file, to be exact, uses the <>.

With that, you're done creating your first-ever library!

Step 4: Adding an Example to Your Arduino Library

We've also learned how adding new libraries to your Arduino IDE can result in new additions to pre-existing examples. The question now is, how do we get our own library to do the same?

Examples aren't just ready pieces of code for you to try and test out. When it comes to the developer part of the spectrum (which you're currently on since it's your very own library that you're designing), you'll understand that Examples are essentially an introduction of your library. If you carried out some of the tasks mentioned previously in the book alongside us, you might already have some experience with examples and thus know the value that they bring to the table, and now, it's your turn to do the same for your own project.

Adding an example to your library isn't exactly a hard task; rather, it's the opposite. You'll have to start off by creating a folder dedicated to examples within your library folder. For us, the library folder was named "ownlibrary" (we understand it isn't the peak of creativity, but it does the job), and we'll assume you have followed suit. Once your *Examples* folder is created within the ownlibrary folder, you just have to add the whole Arduino project file for each example that you want your library to have.

For example, you can simply create a folder within the *Examples* directory called sum, and within the sum folder, you can create an Arduino project called sum.ino. Within the sum file, simply copy-paste the final program1.ino sketch we ended up with during the last section, which looked like:

```
1  #include <ownlibrary.h>
2  void setup()
3  {
4      Serial.begin(9600);
5      int result = sum(4,3);
6      Serial.println(result);
7  }
8  void loop() {}
```

With that, you're done with setting up your example. Don't see it? Well, close and open your Arduino IDE again! Examples are, after all, an addition to a library, and it makes sense to restart the IDE after adding an Example since the library remains unscanned from the last launch of the IDE.

Once you restart, your example, by the name of *sum*, should show itself in the *Examples* option under the *File* option in the top menu.

You can utilize your example however you like, you could simply click on it and execute it, or you could compile it and upload it to your Arduino board, but most importantly, an example would make it a lot easier for people who want to learn how to make full use of your library.

Finally, after creating your own library, you should try to export it to other people and hosting sites such as GitHub. By doing so, you are contributing back to the community. Provided you make commits and increase the number of libraries as you continue to grow more and more proficient in the language, not only will you rack up an impressive portfolio, but you'll also be able to understand more about Git and GitHub and their importance in a professional setting.

A Precaution to Take When Updating Your Arduino IDE

After all your hard work, that is, downloading libraries according to your choice and even creating your own libraries from scratch, surely you wouldn't want all of your accumulated work to go to waste?

Well, losing all your work isn't that far-fetched if you think about a certain scenario, and no, we're not talking about the potential risks to your hard drive, malware, or any other issues. They are, after all, uncontrollable for the most part; what we're talking about here is something much more innocent, updating your Arduino IDE.

Updating your Arduino IDE, for the most part, is a beneficial and simple process until you update your IDE and suddenly all your libraries turn up missing. In simpler terms, the Arduino IDE starts fresh every time you update the IDE; this doesn't mean all your previous sketches will disappear; no, the project folders remain untouched. However, the library folders aren't that lucky.

Even up to the latest Arduino IDE update, the library folder gets wiped out whenever it takes place. Therefore, you must always update your Arduino IDE manually and only after you take the appropriate precautions firsthand.

A great way to solve this issue is to compress the entire *libraries* folder within the *Sketchbook/Arduino* folder and move it to any other directory. Once the Arduino update is complete, you can decompress the library folder and move the whole *libraries* folder back to the *Sketchbook/Arduino directory*. Of course, if you've installed the latest version of the Arduino IDE, you'll already have another *libraries* folder automatically installed by the IDE. That means it's entirely up to you; you can copy or paste the files from your current *libraries* folder to the new one, or you can delete the new *libraries* folder and just move the older directory back to its original place.

Chapter 6

An Introduction to Strings

S trings are basically used to store texts. When you think about it, with the knowledge we've studied until now, we haven't really uncovered how programming languages are able to store whole blocks of texts; surely, they don't use a different variable for every letter; after all, a variable such as *char* can only hold a single value, if you're getting the hang of it then, you're absolutely correct, this is exactly where strings come in to solve the dilemma.

Strings help to record user input and are also used to display text in the Arduino IDE or even on screens. Strings are similar in working to an array, which is simply a collection of similar types of data; you can also think of a string as a fancy word for an array that only holds text data.

In Arduino programming, you can utilize two types of strings:

1. The first and perhaps the one that is more widely used is the Arduino string; it is unique in the fact that it allows room for sketching

2. The second is just the standard string, which is an array of text/characters (depending on how you look at it).

Let's take a deeper look at each of them.

Strings (Character Arrays)

We've already established the fact that a string is a collection of characters. You can call it an array of characters in more sophisticated or programming-oriented terms. Look at the example below to get a clearer idea of a string.

```
1  char str[]="Hello World";
2  void setup()
3 ▾ {
4    Serial.begin(9600);
5    void setup();
6    Serial.println(str);
7  }
8  void loop() {}
9
```

As shown in line 1, a string must be defined by writing out the data type along with its name and two square brackets; the two square brackets here are of the utmost importance. After all, they are really what signifies the declaration of a string, and they are also what cements its place as a type of array.

Aside from the string, the snippet above is just a standard Arduino program. Finally, you can also print your string to the serial monitor using a function we've already used before, SerialprintIn(), where the name of the string goes inside the parenthesis.

How Do You Manipulate Strings?

Strings aren't just popular for storing texts; they can be altered and tinkered with in various ways, making them very useful to have around in almost every programming language, not just Arduino. You can tinker with a string within your sketch using some of the techniques shown below, or if you're curious enough, you can also go around on your own investigative spree to figure out other ways and functions that will help you achieve the same tasks.

Strings are based on an index pattern. This means that every character you store in a string is assigned an index number that starts from 0 and can extend up to anywhere as much as the storage space allocated to the string allows. This may be hard for you to understand in words, but a little example should do the trick for you:

Let's take the example of the "str" string we created in the code snippet above. The str was used to save the "Hello World" text. Going by our explanation of strings and their mechanisms above, each word starting from the H in "Hello World" is assigned an index number in ascending order starting from 0 to, in this case, 11 with H being the 0, e being the one and so on. Even the spaces between the words are assigned an index number.

These index numbers are then referred to whenever a string is called. You can think of them as a reference number for where the value of the character is stored in the string. Since each index stores only one individual character, this leaves a lot of room for flexibility with the string. For instance, you can change the individual characters of the string by mentioning the index number and the new value for that specific index number; you can look at the code below to better understand. In this scenario, continuing on from the previous example, let's change the hello in "Hello World" to Heylo; it will only take a single line of code!

```
1    char str[]="Hello World";
2    void setup()
3 ▾  {
4    Serial.begin(9600);
5    void setup();
6    Serial.println(str);
7    str[2]='y';
8
9    }
10   void loop() {}
```

The only difference from the previous code snippet in the example above is the addition at line 8. As we already mentioned, to change a specific character within a string, you just have to mention the index number of the character within the square brackets and the new value to be assigned to the specific index number. Of course, you should probably check your program to see whether your alteration works; do you know how you can go around doing it?

If you came up with the idea to print the new value of the string again by using the *Serial.printIn()* function, then you're absolutely correct. Printing out your values to see whether they're exactly as you expect them to be is the primary method of checking whether your program is working as it should or not. Furthermore, it isn't only beginners who employ this trick; it is a simple yet very powerful tactic to find out where the error in your program lies. Many advanced programmers tend to use the print function at regular intervals throughout their program to check where their values go wrong and to pinpoint the exact location of the error.

Also, as you might have already guessed or even tried out by yourself at this point, you can replace entire words in the string as per your liking by copy-pasting the same line above over and over again for each and every index of the string, of course, this isn't exactly efficient since it takes a lot of space to accomplish a simple task; this won't cause much of an issue for you during short programs such as these, after all an increase of a few lines won't prolong compilation time by much, however, during larger programs, this can cause a lot of issues since it not only increases the compilation time of the program, but it also makes the program much heavier in size.

This is where loops come in; with loops, you can move through indexes one by one and change them as you like, and you can accomplish it with minimal lines of code and a highly efficient program is born.

What Are Some Commonly Used Functions to Manipulate Strings?

We've covered the basics of strings and their manipulation. If we look at strings as a whole, although the single character index assignment leaves room for a lot of flexibility, replacing the values with the index is just scratching the surface.

Now that that's out of the way, let's move on to the topic at hand, strings and functions. If you think about it, with all the possibilities that strings promise, it'd be unnatural for a string not to have any dedicated functions to help in manipulating them.

Suppose you're a C language enthusiast (**Reminder:** the Arduino language is based on C++; thus, it has a very close relationship with

Java and C). some of these functions might seem vaguely familiar to you; after all, these functions are a part of libraries that predominantly belong to the C language.

- **Function to print strings**

We've already discussed the printing function a bit. The Serial.printIn() function is the go-to function for developers to print out their code, be it values of variables or whole strings.

You can print out whole strings using the print function. However, it isn't just limited to that; you can also print out a specific index of the string. All you have to do is to mention the index number in the square bracket along with the name of the string in the parenthesis of the print function, it should look something like this if we take the previous example: *Serial.printIn(str[2])*.

- **Function to determine the length of strings**

The string length function is used to determine the length of the string. It is quite useful, especially if you're trying to determine the number of times your loop will run or the current size/value of the string in question.

You can use the *strlen()* function to find out the length of any string. You have to be careful of one thing; however, the strlen() function exists solely to perform its own task; if you intend to use the value returned from the strlen function later on in your program, you'll have to store it in a variable or if you want to print out the value that the function returns, you'll either have to use the strlen() function within the print function *Serial.printIn(str[2])* or you'd have to store the value returned from the strlen() function within a variable and print the variable, later on, something you've already learned to do at this point.

- **Function to determine the length of the string range**

The sizeof() function is also used to get the length of a string. Now, you might be wondering why a string needs two functions to perform the same task, and if you think there's a catch, you're right! While it might seem like the sizeof() and the strlength() functions carry out the same task at a glance, there'll be a slight difference between the values the two return depending on certain conditions.

Another key difference between the two is their nature. Strlen() is a fully-fledged function; on the other hand, while sizeof() might seem like a function() it is actually otherwise, sizeof() is an operator.

Typically, the length returned by the sizeof() operator is of a higher value than the strlen() function; this is because the sizeof() function also includes the null terminator when it determines the count of a string.

The null terminator, which is signified by the 0 code in ASCII (the American Standard Code for Information Interchange), is a reserved character in Arduino that actually signifies the end of a string; many of the standard string functions in the language (Arduino) rely on the null terminator which includes the strlen(), strcpy() and the strcmp() function too. Now that you're familiar with the definition of the null terminator, can you guess what would happen if the null terminator wasn't included? Since the null terminator tells functions where a string ends, without it, the function would continue way beyond the string to read subsequent bytes of data/memory that weren't even a part of the string. To set a null terminator in a string, you just have to assign 0 to the final index value you want the function to read. For example, for the str function, we can use *str [11] = 0;* (**Tip:** Remember the difference between 0 and '0' the first one is the integer 0 which is used to signal a null terminator at that specific index place, the latter is 0 in the form of a string which will act just like any other character in a string would).

Furthermore, sizeof() is also not a part of the conventional C string library, and its main purpose is to determine the difference in length between the length of the string and the length of the range of the string (the range includes the null function too).

- **Concatenation**

Concatenation in English means linking two or more things together; in Arduino, the definition isn't far from the original English language; it simply means adding two strings into one.

String concatenation is a sketch that joins two strings together; it isn't complex but the exact opposite. The concatenation can be achieved by just using the string() function. The additional chain feature pulls together the second string and chains it to the back of the first, thereby linking/concatenating the two strings.

Just like the strlen() function, during concatenation, the function returns a value that must be stored in a new string (it can be stored in an older one, too, if you do not intend to use them any longer). The point is, the value must be stored or made use of at the same time as when the function is called otherwise your newly concatenated string will not be stored anywhere.

You can check whether your concatenation has been successful by printing the new string using the print function, or you could print out the value of its length and compare it with the length of the first two strings (it should be somewhere around the total of the two strings).

- **The string's selection bounds**

Did you know you can actually set the character limit of a string during the time of its declaration? In simpler terms, along with the declaration of a string, you can also define how many characters get to be stored within the string. It isn't really that hard; all you have to do is to specify a number within the square brackets during the declaration of the string, for example:

A normal string declaration goes like this:

```
char str[]= 'Hello World"
```

A string with a set limit would have a syntax of:

```
char str[11]= 'Hello World'
```

At this point, the second string does not have any space left to store another character; thus, any character inside the string can only be replaced and not be added to.

Arduino String (Object String)

Until now, we've only discussed the first type of string, the second type of string is known as the object string (otherwise also known as the Arduino string), and it can be used in sketching as well.

What Does the Object in Object String Stand For?

An object in programming, or rather Arduino, is simply a construct that contains not only data (just like normal functions) but functions as well.

An object string can be used and manipulated just like a normal string can be; it can also be produced like a variable and assigned a single value. What sets it apart from the normal string is its features; these features target the information contained within the string and are quite useful. If you're familiar with the concepts of OOP (Object Oriented Programming), you'll recognize these features as they're normally referred to as "approaches" in OOP terminology.

A string object is declared more like a variable than an array; you can declare a string variable if you just remove the square bracket and use "" instead of the " during the string array declaration. If you were wondering, these "approaches" or functions are called upon using the name of the String object and a "." and then the name of the function; we'll take you through some examples later. Once created, you can use multiple string object functions; you can find a proper list of all the functions that a String class has to offer by going through the Arduino String Reference. We will, however, be looking at a few of the functions that belong to the string class, which includes functions such as:

- **Changing your string to uppercase letters**

Out of the many functions a string object has, there is a function to change all the characters inside the string object and capitalize them. The function is known as toUppercase() and works only on string objects. This function targets only the string information and turns every character into its uppercase version. As for characters that are already uppercase, the function leaves them be. You can call upon the function with the name of the String object and the dot operator along with the name of the function; for example, *str.toUpper()* would change "Hello World" to "HELLO WORLD".

- **Getting the length of your string**

Unlike the function we previously discussed, getting the length of your string object is actually pretty easy. You just have to add the .length() extension to your string name, and BOOM! You'll have the length of your string object. Just like the strlen() function, you'll have to pass the retuning value on to a variable or directly into the print function.

When Is a String Object Usable?

After familiarizing yourself with string objects, declaring new objects, and trying some of their associated functions, what do you think is a more efficient and preferable option?

While we certainly don't speak for every Arduino programmer out there, it is but a fact that most Arduino programmers, especially those who have progressed onto the intermediate and perhaps advanced stages of the programming language, prefer to use string objects rather than the more traditional string array approach. This is because an object has a higher number of integrated functions that can be used seamlessly and are considered far more professional. However, just because strong objects are considered a superior option (by a majority of the people using Arduino) doesn't mean that they're always used; this is because while a string object is much easier to use, it also has its own disadvantages.

The most major downside and perhaps one which discourages many users from opting to create string objects is that it takes a great deal of memory to operate. Whenever you create a string object, it takes a large part of your memory and can rapidly deplete the RAM of your Arduino board when you upload your sketch to the board; this can cause your Arduino program to lag, hang up for an unknown period of time and may even cause it to crash entirely (**Reminder:** You won't actually lose any of your progress when this happens. After all, whenever you have to upload a sketch, you have to save your program first; you can think of it as a failsafe to protect a user's progress whenever a program crashes).

However, there won't really be a problem if you act smartly and use objects only if you intend to make heavy use of that particular string later on. Another downside of using up too much RAM is that even if your program doesn't crash and your sketch gets uploaded to your Arduino board, there'll be a visible strain on the board itself, and some commands might take a long while to execute. This delay is quite perceptible; that is, you'll be able to see the time difference in execution between a program that runs on string arrays entirely and a program that runs entirely on string objects.

Also, the visible strain on your board or your program freezing up/hanging from overuse of string objects becomes much more prominent or recurring in Arduino boards that fall on the shorter end of the RAM-size spectrum. A prime example of such an Arduino board is the Arduino UNO (**Reminder:** It is understandable for the Arduino UNO's RAM to be unable to handle a large number of string objects since it was mainly meant for beginners).

String arrays are more commonly known as character arrays. There is a little technicality in the names here. A string array would stand for an array that contains a string on every one of its indexes (**Reminder:** A string is a sequence of characters that are grouped together); on the other hand, a character array would refer to an array that has a character on each and every one of its indexes which would ultimately make the whole array a string once its characters were grouped together. Was it a little hard to understand? Read the paragraph from beginning to end, one sentence at a time, and create a mind map after contemplating at the end of each sentence.

From this point forward, we'll interchange the words character arrays and string arrays. The only problem with character arrays is that they're a lot harder to use. Furthermore, unlike an object, when using a string array, you may not always be able to find a function that suits your tastes or a function that will be able to perform your required task. In such a scenario, you might end up having to compose your own function. While this may be a hassle, you do end up having a lot more control over your string than if you opted for an object.

When using character arrays, you have total control over what size the string you make has. You can make a string short to save up on your RAM's processing power, or you can go big if you have a board capable of withstanding it, everything depends on you, on the other hand, do remember that if string objects bring a certain level of comfort with them with their preexisting functions, they also occupy space/memory of a similar level.

With character arrays, and this is something we have discussed before, you should always remember to respect the boundaries of your string. You should never try to employ different string varieties to impose beyond the range of your character arrays. String objects do not have such a problem. In fact, when you use string objects, the object itself will take care of the string boundaries for you (you have to rest easy and leave everything to your declared object). Unlike character arrays, object strings do not rewrite on the end of the string in question (or, in other words, the string in operation). Rather, it can use write and manipulate memory for the string to operate when it runs short of space.

At the end of the day, the choice is yours; if you have a board that has a limited amount of RAM, then using object strings sparingly and opting for character strings that give you much more control over your memory usage is optimal, however, if you have enough RAM on your hands to be extravagant then using an object definitely won't hurt and will actually ease up your programming journey a bit.

Chapter 7

Functions in Arduino

Functions allow a programmer to reuse sections of code within their program without the need to repeat an entire block of code again and again; this is done by calling the function again. Functions make your program much more efficient and allow you to save a lot of space when it comes to larger programs. Furthermore, when you structure your program in small/large sectors of code, it leaves a professional impression and will generally leave your code much tidier in comparison to simply repeating your code over and over again.

Until now, we've only indirectly discussed functions, whether it be through libraries or showing you how to manipulate character arrays; however, now that you're quite familiar with most of the other Arduino technologies, we think it's time to get you familiarized with perhaps the building block of the Arduino language or programming in general.

Just think about it, what makes all of the things we've studied up to this point actually useful? Take your time; what do libraries and strings (whether it be object strings or character strings) have in common that makes them so useful? Maybe the name of the topic we're discussing is already something of a cheat, so if you came to the answer "Functions," you're absolutely right.

Now that you think about it, libraries are essentially a collection of objects/classes; what are objects essentially made up of? Functions. What about strings? Well, strings are mighty convenient because they allow you to store multiple characters at a time, which you can use to display words or even short sentences, but think about what would you do with a string if there weren't any functions to manipulate said strings? It would be a hassle just to print your string out, let alone some of the more complex tasks if it weren't for functions. Finally, if you reuse code instead of functions, if an error occurs in your reused code, you'll have to fix the error at multiple locations, whereas if you use a function, you just have to make adjustments at the function declaration location of your program.

We hope that this is enough to get you to use strings. At this point, we've already shown you how to declare a function (**Reminder:**

Refer to **How to Create Your own Libraries -> Step 1: Writing a Program** section of the book); however, it was only a glimpse into the code, and we didn't offer any real explanations since there is a whole topic dedicated to functions and their uses.

There are two basic functions in Arduino sketches, the setup() and the loop() function. If you remember, during the **"How to Create a Library?"** section of the book, we introduced you to both of these functions and mentioned that their use would be explained later. Well, what better time than now?

The Setup() and the Loop() Function

Whenever you create a new Arduino sketch, you're presented with a file that already has some lines of code written in it; these lines of code are there to make sure that you're able to access all of the basic Arduino functionalities and that your program is understood by your compiler.

Within these lines of code are the two basic pre-defined functions, the loop() and the setup() function. Any function aside from these two must be called with a library, or they should be declared manually. Let's take a look at each of these functions separately.

The Setup() Function

The setup() function is the bane of all the programming that takes place in your sketch. Without the setup() function, your sketch would be deprived of its basic ability to infer an Arduino program, which is why the Arduino IDE includes it whenever an entirely new program is created.

The setup function defines the Arduino state on boot and runs the program set in place for a more compact definition. You can carry out everything within the scope of the setup() function, which includes but is not limited to. Initializing variables and classes, specifying pin functionality (by using a function known as the pinMode()) and you can also set define the preliminary pin state within the setup() function.

The setup() function is referred to/called whenever you start a program or whenever you shut down or restart the program or the IDE.

The Loop() Function

After the setup() function, the loop() function is the second most important in Arduino. Like the former, each program must have a loop() function to work and perform normally.

Loop() is a primary function that, as the name might hint, executes your program over and over in a loop() which helps to explain the basic principles for your circuit.

With that, we've taken a look at the two primary functions needed to manipulate any program in Arduino. However, that isn't all that functions in Arduino have to offer. In the topics that follow, we'll take a look at declaring a function yourself along with some of the built-in functions in the Arduino IDE, and we'll also look at the SD library, which is mainly associated with manipulating an SD card and is applicable to microcontrollers that have a micro-SD card slot on their board.

Arduino's Integrated I/O Functions

Digital I/O Functions

There are many Arduino functions dedicated to handling the input and output processes of your Arduino gadget; these include:

DigitalRead()

The DigitalRead() function is used to check/verify the values from a digital pin. The function only accepts a PIN as a parameter, and in return, it returns a consistent (which can either be LOW or HIGH).

DigitalWrite()

You can think of DigitalWrite() as the polar opposite of the DigitalRead() function. Where Digital read accepts a PIN to return a consistent, when using the DigitalWrite() function, you have to assign the PIN and the consistent yourself, which can then be assigned to a digital output pin.

PinMode()

We've already mentioned the PinMode function a few times before. The PinMode() function determines the nature of the pin. When using the function, you can set the nature of a pin to be input or output according to what you'd prefer it to be. If you want to use the PinMode function, you'll have to pass the PIN along with your preferred choice, INPUT or OUTPUT, to set your pin.

There are also other digital I/O functions such as the pulseIn() and the ShiftIn() and ShiftOut() functions. The former is used to read a pulse, whereas the latter is used to manipulate a byte of data/information from/to a pin. Aside from these, when you set about researching by yourself, you'll be greeted with an even greater number of digital I/O functions, which is only natural after all; Arduino has been present for a long time. However, you don't need to worry as you gradually get more comfortable with Arduino; you'll also learn to manipulate these functions.

Analog I/O Functions

As you might have already guessed, based on the pattern, the purpose or the task achieved by a function is often self-explanatory due to its name. This is because whoever contributed the function followed proper naming conventions, which helps -others who use a function, such as you, to figure out its use without even referring to the documentation.

AnalogRead()

The AnalogRead() function is used to read the Analog value. The wave produced for the analog value is often formed on the button.

AnalogReadResolution()

The AnalogReadResolution() allows you to tamper with the default bit resolution set by the AnalogRead() function. The value is set at 10 bits by default, which works great with most of the Arduino devices you'll use in your preliminary coding stages. However, once you progress to more advanced coding, your sketches are then designed to work with some more complex Arduino microcontrollers such as the MKR and the Arduino fee. That means you'll have to resort to using the AnalogReadResolution() to change the default bit resolution to make sure that your program runs seamlessly without any error.

AnalogWrite()

This function is used to write an analog rate to the pin on your board. It isn't anything complex. However, it is quite vital when it comes to programming a board according to the task you must accomplish.

AnalogWriteResolution()

Similar to the AnalogReadResolution(), the AnalogWriteResolution() function also allows you to tamper with the bit resolution assigned by default to AnalogWrite(), which is, once again, by default, set to 10 bits. This function only deals with specific gadgets such as the MKR, ZERO, and the Arduino Charge.

Arduino's Time Functions

Sometimes, the project you're working on might have special requirements, for example, executing your sketch at a specific time (much like the night light sketch we discussed in earlier chapters), or your sketch might just require a small delay before execution. In such cases, Arduino's time functions would be sufficient to help you out. Some of the more commonly used time functions in Arduino include:

Delay()

The delay() function is perhaps the most popular out of all of Arduino's integrated time functions among newbies. The delay() function is used to stop the Arduino program/sketch (whatever you prefer to call it at this point, the term sketch is more preferred as it is inclusive to Arduino and signifies your belonging to the community). When using the delay() function, you get the opportunity to put a break of a number of milliseconds wherever you want within your program. You can specify the period of the break within the parameters of the delay() function.

There are other variations of the delay function, too; let's take, for example, the **DelayMicroSeconds()** function; this function has the same exact usage as the delay() function, even the parameters are the same! The only difference, which you might have already pointed out from the name, is that where the delay() function delays the program for a specific number of milliseconds, the latter delays the function for a specified amount of micro-seconds.

Micros()

The micros function in Arduino is used to obtain the number of microseconds that the program has spent in action. It returns a value (in microseconds) that specifies the amount of time (in microseconds, that a program has run). However, you have to be careful when using this function; after all, the Micros() function resets its value after ~70 minutes because the memory/space allocated to the function overflows. Hence, the function restarts the count from 0.

Another variation of the Micros() function is the **Millis()** function. There are a few differences in how both of the functions operate. The Millis() function returns the time (in milliseconds) at the time when your Arduino board beings to run your sketch. Like the

Micros() function, the Millis() function also resets after its memory/space overflows. The time to overflow for the Millis() function is way longer than if you opt for the Micros function(); on average, the Millis() function returns to zero (or, in other words, overflows) after a period of 50 days.

Arduino's Mathematical Functions

Having basic mathematical functions integrated is a must for any Integrated Development Environment, and the same goes for the Arduino IDE. After all, if you think about it for a while, coding and mathematics are closely connected. Now, if you had to resort to writing your own function every time you wanted to carry out a simple mathematical task, it would cost you not only a lot of time and effort, but it'd also leave take a lot of your attention off from the main sketch at hand; this is why the Arduino IDE has a range of mathematical functions you can use to simplify a lot of your tasks, these include functions such as:

Max()

The Max() function takes in integer values as its parameters and returns whatever has a higher value. It is great for distinguishing between inputs and returning whatever input has a higher value. The polar opposite of the max() function is the min() function; just like the max() function, the min() function also takes in two integer values in its parameters and returns whichever value it judges to be the smaller out of the lot.

Sq()

If you're getting the hang of determining a function's use just by its name, you might have already guessed what the sq() function is used for.

The sq() function is used to find out the square of any integer you enter into the parameters. It is quite a straightforward function and wouldn't be much of an issue to create even by yourself. However, using a single sq() (and parameters within) is still more convenient than writing out 2-3 extra lines of code.

Reverse Functions

Now, at this stage, you might have noticed something already. Most of the functions we've studied up until this point follow a specific pattern, which is much truer for mathematical functions than the other types. Most functions have a reverse function of themselves. In simpler terms, most functions have a counterpart function that carries out the exact opposite of the task that they themselves were meant to carry out.

For example, the reverse function of the max() function we studied earlier would be the min() function, where the max() finds out the maximum value from two integers, and the min() function tells the minimum value of the two. Likewise, the sq() function also has a reverse function; can you guess what it might be?

If you guessed that the reverse function has something to do with finding the square root of a number, you're absolutely right! The

Sqrt() function is used to find the square root of whatever value you put inside the parameter.

Sin(), Cos() and Tan()

You might be familiar with these three functions if you've studied basic geometry. These three functions are primarily used to deal with angles. The cos, sin, and tan functions are used to find an angle's cosine, sine, and tangent.

Arduino Number Generators

There are multiple scenarios in which you might have to generate a random number. If we're talking purely on the basis of programming, by using a random number generator, you can create a small guess-game where a user will have to guess a number between a specified range. That number will be generated randomly by your function. We'll take a look at some of such functions below, and then we'll also look at a similar function inclined more towards Arduino.

Random()

The random() function, similar to what we discussed above, is used to generate a random number. While the random number does not really need a parameter, if you want the function to generate a pseudo-random number from a specified range, you'll have to use the parameters to specify your range; for instance, if we take the guessing game above, trying to guess any number between 0-10 would make a short but interesting game.

RandomSeed()

The randomseed() function is a little more unique in comparison to the random() function. The function is used to initialize a random number creator by using a random first figure. Like many other programming languages today, you can't get completely random numbers; whether using the preexisting functions or making your own, the numbers generated out of either will always follow something of a pattern. Hence, to solve the issue, the number generator is seeded with another value, for example, something like the current time, or if we're speaking strictly in Arduino terms, checking out the input value from the analog port would be a far better and a more viable option.

Disrupt Functions in Arduino

There are many functions in Arduino that allow you to manipulate disrupts and interrupts. Using specific functions (which we'll discuss later), you can disable disrupts throughout a program or enable a disrupt again; you can even attach a disrupt or an interrupt wherever you feel like it! Let's learn exactly what sort of functions are used to accomplish said tasks:

NoInterrupts()

The nointerrupts() function does exactly what the name specifies; that is, it disables interrupts throughout a program.

Disrupts()

Now, this is a prime example of the reverse function ideology we set out to make you understand. Using the Disrupts() function, you can re-enable disrupts that have been disabled throughout a program.

AttachInterrupt()

The attachinterrupt() function allows you to mess with a digital input pin. Using the attachinterrupt() function, you can use an interrupt to disrupt a digital input of your liking, provided that it is one of the permitted pins. To look up more about the permitted pins on your board and where you can use the attachinterrupt() function, you'll have to look it up using the primary documentation of your board.

DetachInterrupt()

You might have already seen this coming with everything we've studied until now. The function we're going to discuss right after the attachinterrupt() is the detachinterrupt() function, which sets out to do the exact opposite of what the former function did.

The detachinterrupt() function is solely used to finish the interrupt that was set using the attachinterrupt() function. To use this function, you don't even have to look up the primary docs, as it won't work unless the attachinterrupt() function has been successful. If you're a beginner, which is what we'll assume since you're reading this book, you probably won't have to use functions that aren't already a part of Arduino. For beginners, we recommend familiarizing yourself with functions already within Arduino and then moving on to using functions from the outside library. Now that you're familiar with most of the built-in functions that Arduino already offers, let's move into a little more detail regarding function declaration and calling.

Function Declaration

Whenever a function is created, it is always declared solely. In simpler terms, a function must be declared outside the body of any other function, and this includes even the two main functions we discussed above, namely the setup() and loop(). If you might remember, we didn't mention function declaration when we discussed everything that the setup() function allows you to do.

Alternatively, you can also refer to the snippet of the program in **How to Create Your own Library -> Writing a Program**. In the snippet, the sum() function was declared outside of any other boundaries at the top of the program and was then called within the setup(). (**Reminder:** You cannot declare a function within the setup() function; however, you are allowed to call your declared function within setup()).

You can declare a function by using the following syntax:

Function-Return-Type name-of-the-function()

{

This is where the task performed by the function is specified. Each line of this task is followed by a semicolon (;), which specifies the end of a line in Arduino. (**Reminder:** Pressing enter does not specify where a line breaks in Arduino! Instead, if you want the compiler to know where your line ends, you'll have to use a semicolon (;) which makes the compiler treat the two lines before and after the semicolon differently)

```
}
```

You can compare this format to the sum() function that we created in the library section. Furthermore, while the parenthesis is used to signify a function, during declaration, they're also used to set the parameters that will be needed when the function is called.

During function declaration, you have to mention the parameters to be called and the type of parameters the function will use. If we were to refer to the sum() function once again, you could clearly see the int x and int y defined clearly within the parenthesis of the sum() function.

Also, the function return type that you set must match the return value from the function itself. Just like in the sum() example, we set the return type to integer (int sum(int x, int y)) if you remember, and the return x + y; part of the program returned an integer value too. If we tried to return a character value, for example, return a; it would result in an error, and the function would be unable to work properly.

Finally, once you're done defining the sum() functioning and all the tasks it must accomplish, you just have to call the function. Calling a function is fairly straightforward. You can call a function directly by mentioning its name and satisfying all the parameters that you set during declaration. (**Reminder:** When calling a function, all of the values that you enter into the parenthesis must be in the same order and of the same type as the parameters you during the function declaration, for example, if you set int x and char y, then when you call a function, you must first specify the value of x and then y and not the other way around; also, the value of x must be an integer, and the value of y must be a char. Otherwise, you will face an error when executing your program; after all, an int parameter can only store an integer value, whereas a char parameter can only store a single character value).

However, as you might remember (since this is something we've discussed multiple times beforehand), just calling your function won't give you the ability to manipulate the value returned from the function. To make use of the value returning from the function, you'll have to store the returning value in a variable and then use it accordingly, or you'll have to call the function directly within another function.

With that, we're almost done with functions! However, don't go around celebrating just yet. After all, we still have the final topic to go. In this subtopic, we won't be discussing anything new related to functions. Rather, since we've discussed built-in functions, we'll look at functions that belong to a specific library, a library that will be of great use to your further on in your Arduino programming career.

Chapter 8

Arrays in Arduino

We've already discussed a lot about arrays previously. In simple terms, an array is a group or collection of values strung together; these values are of the same data type. We've learned about character/string arrays; however, they aren't the only arrays in the Arduino programming language. Just like you can create string arrays, you can create arrays of almost every data type. An array can be created with the following declaration:

Data-type array-name[*array-size*];

The data type defines the type of values you want to store in your array. For instance, if you create an integer array, you'll only be able to store integer values within the array and nothing else; similarly, character/string arrays can only store character values.

When it comes to the array name, following proper naming conventions is a choice; that is, you can name your array something that points out its purpose in the program, for example, if you want to store the names of students in a class the array should be named something along the lines of student_name. However, you can also name the array something convenient but completed unrelated, for example, "a." It's up to you. However, it is better to train yourself to follow proper naming conventions from an early age in your programming career, it will be of great help to you later on when you transition onto a professional stage.

There isn't really much to discuss when it comes to arrays in Arduino. You can treat all other types of arrays just like the string arrays. For different types of arrays, you'll be able to find different types of libraries and functions that cater to them. Just like string arrays, all arrays store a single value on each of their indexes which can be printed out using a loop, or you could print out all of the values together too.

Arrays are a complex part of Arduino programming and are often only introduced in the latter stages. However, since this is a book revolving around the techniques to get more efficient at Arduino programming, introducing you to array is a key point. With arrays, you get to forego making multiple variables of a single type; you can just declare an array, and that's it.

Arrays are complex to handle; however, if you just respect the basic rules of an array (something we taught you back when we were discussing character arrays, for example, not exceeding the set boundary of a string array), then you'll find that your array journey will actually be pretty seamless with a lot to learn.

Chapter 9

The Arduino Due and USB Host

A USB host (also known as a USB on-the-go) was a feature introduced all the way back in 2001, even before the Arduino programming language or platform was even landed. The feature allowed devices with USB specifications to act as a host, a host which would then allow other devices such as a mouse or keyboard to be connected to itself.

For any USB device to work, it must be connected to the main device, also known as the USB host; otherwise, it won't work. Before the introduction of a USB host, it was a hassle to connect devices to the main device; let's take a PC, for example. Back in the day, PCs had a limited number of ports that could be used for connectivity; hence, you almost always had to buy extensions if you really wanted to enjoy your PC. After all, original floppy disks didn't have that much space. Therefore, you had to acquire a pluggable external disk drive too, which offered a lot more space, couple that with a mouse, keyboard, printer, or scanner, and you almost always had to forego one device for another. However, when USB connectivity (or on-the-go) was introduced, everything changed.

An Introduction to USB Devices and the Arduino Due

Even if you're not that tech-savvy, you must be familiar with the main USB devices in use today. These devices include the commonly used keyboard, mice, and hubs (although they aren't as commonly found as they used to be before).

Why are we discussing these basic devices? Well, it's because this chapter focuses on the Arduino Due, which by itself is a USB host. Are you getting it? Since the Arduino Due is a USB host, it means you can connect your keyboard, mice, and hub to the Due and manipulate it with the connected devices.

An Introduction to Arduino Due

We didn't discuss the Arduino Due along with the other Arduino devices for many reasons. One of them is that the Due is vastly different from any of the other devices we mentioned before. The Arduino Due is based on Atmel's SAM3X8E, which is quite a powerful microcontroller. It also has around two micro-USB connectors.

Without getting into much detail, it'd be sufficient to know that the Due is a USB host with full control of its USB port; thus, this port can be used as a slave when attempting native serial communication. Not only that, but the Arduino due is also compatible with USB OTG; thus, it can be used to connect with other USB devices such as mice and keyboards and hence also receive input from them. Now, this brings us to a question you might have been wondering, how exactly does this happen?

The Arduino Due is capable of using the USBHost library. This library is extremely powerful and contains many routines that can be triggered by USB devices such as a keyboard and mice. However, since USB drivers are quite big, the Arduino Due can only take input from one device at a time, whether it be a keyboard or a mouse. The topic that we're discussing is based entirely on the Arduino Due and how we can use the USBHost library to manipulate the Due using input from these USB devices.

Using the USBHost Library

If you're using Arduino version 1.5 or later, you'll already have the USBHost library preinstalled. In such a case, all you have to do is to import the library from the sketch menu. If you're using another version, you already know how to install libraries manually at this point.

After importing the USBHost library, you'll see that a large number of libraries have been imported in your sketch (these are all libraries that the USBHost library is dependent upon).

To gain access to everything the library offers, you'll have to create an object after initializing the USB controller. An object can be created by writing out the following code in your Arduino IDE.

USBHost obj;

obj.task();

The task() is helpful when it comes to processing USB events. Whenever you use the task(), it waits for a USB event to occur; whenever it does, the task() calls upon the necessary function for the event to occur without a hitch. The task() allows no other function to run while it is running, and if it detects no USB events within five seconds, the function returns and does not wait any further for a time-out.

Using a Keyboard with the Arduino Due

If you want to use a keyboard with the Arduino Due, you'll have to define the keyboard controller class (yes, the keyboard has its own controller class). It isn't much; all you have to do is:

USBHost obj;

KeyboardController kb(obj);

And there you have it! Now, when you initialize this class, it'll call two functions whenever a specific event occurs: pressing and releasing a key. These events are not called upon when a modifier key is pressed, for example, shift, alt, or tab (however, it is called whenever caps lock is pressed).

The two functions, i.e., the keyReleased() and the keyPressed() functions, do not need to have any sort of parameter input. Instead, they get their input from other sources.

Once you've created your keyboard controller object, you can manipulate your keyboard in several ways. For example, these two functions tell the sketch that a key has been released or has been pressed; however, you can also get to know which key it was with a little extra effort.

To get to know the key that was pressed, you'll have to use the getKey() function. The getKey() function returns the ASCII code of the key that you've pressed; you can store the value of the ASCII code in another variable entirely. If we were to continue to above code as an example, to get the ASCII code of the *kb* object, we'd have to write down the following code:

code = kb.getKey()

However, you should remember that not every key on the keyboard has a corresponding ASCII value which is why using the getOemKey() function is a far more superior alternative.

Unlike the Ascii code, the getOemKey() obtains the OEM code which every character on the keyboard has, and thus, you do not have to worry about the function not working; that is, not unless you're trying to get whether a modifier key has been pressed. If you want to figure out the status of modifier keys (such as shift, alt, tab, etc.), you'll have to use the getModifiers() functions. This function returns an integer value that can be used to determine the modifier key pressed. You can refer to the table below for modifier keys and their corresponding integer values:

Modifier Key	Integer Value
LeftCtrl	1
RightCtrl	16
Alt	4
LeftShift	2
RightShift	32
AltGr	64
LeftCmd	8
RightCmd	128

Using Mice with the Arduino Due

Mice, like the keyboard, are quite easy to use; all you have to do is create a mouse controller similarly to how you created a keyboard controller.

USBHost obj;

MouseController mc(obj);

With that, you've created your mouse controller, and you can use the mouse to manipulate the USB host using the functions in your sketch. The mouse controller can call four functions, each of which is called under different circumstances, which include: when the mouse button is pushed or released and when the mouse is dragged or moved. The functions for each of these actions are the mousePressed(), mouseReleased(), mouseDragged() and mouseMoved() respectively.

You can do a lot using the mouse controller you've created. For example, you can use the getYChange() and the getXChange() functions to track the movement information of your mouse, which works similar to a graph (with a top-left coordinate system, one that starts from (0,0)), you get the change in coordinates of the position of your mouse.

While there is a lot more to discuss when it comes to how you can manipulate the mouse controller, there's only so much you can do with the knowledge in the beginning stages of your career as a programmer; hence, we will be moving on to the next topic at hand.

Chapter 10

Serial Communication

In computer science, serial communication refers to the data transfer which takes place one bit at a time over a communication bus. We have a lot of examples of Serial bus communication all around us. Can you think of one? (**Hint:** Think of the full form of USB) Still can't get it? The most common example of Serial communication is the USB; the S in USB stands for Serial communication, and the full form of USB is Universal Serial Bus.

Introduction to Serial Communication

There are two main types of communication, Serial and Parallel. Let's look at the differences between them and determine which is the better option.

Serial Communication vs. Parallel Communication

In serial communication, data is sent over 1 bit at a time over a single wire in a single direction. On the other hand, parallel communication is unidirectional and can send over multiple bits at a time using a higher number of channels (each channel still transfers a single bit at a time, only the number of channels has increased).

While parallel communication seems like a faster approach (and it is) since a large number of bits are sent over simultaneously compared to serial transmission (with a ratio of 1:8), it still isn't our final choice when it comes to Arduino programming. Why is this the case?

One reason for this is the number of channels involved in the transfer. Since a higher number of bits are transferred at a time, parallel transfers also require a higher number of channels to be in place. If you think about it this way, serial communication, which only uses a single channel and can only manage a single-way communication at a time, would undoubtedly result in an overall cheaper investment too.

Another reason is that the smaller number of channels also makes propagating them a whole lot easier; fewer channels also result in lesser crosstalk.

The final reason and perhaps the most vital one is the improvement of serial communication over the decades. In the present day, serial communication can reach up to 1 terabit per second. While parallel will still be faster, considering both communications are of the same quality, the difference in speed isn't anything you'd be able to miss, which is what results in serial communication undoubtedly coming out as the winner of the lot.

An Introduction to Serial Protocols

In computer terminology, a protocol is an agreement between two parties (or, in this case, two devices) over how the transfer of data should occur. When it comes to a serial protocol, it is essentially an agreement that the data transfer takes place a bit at a time down a sole channel between the two devices; furthermore, at the same time, only one of the devices acts as a sender whereas the other acts as a receiver.

While we won't discuss serial protocols in this book, we'll at least provide you with the types of serial protocols that are commonly used so that you'll be able to search them up and read up on them yourself. Serial protocols contain many logical concepts that'll help you later on in your Arduino career. Examples of the most common serial protocols include:

1. **The Morse Code Telegraphy Protocol:** It is one of the oldest serial protocols available; it can send words, operators, and a lot of other information by sending short and long pulses with blanks in between.

2. **The USB:** We've discussed a lot about the USB in this book. Once again, the importance of the USB is highlighted, only this time as a serial protocol that holds its worth against other protocols.

3. **The SPI:** Does the term SPI seem vaguely familiar? Well, that's because it has been mentioned multiple times throughout the book. The SPI (also known as the Serial Peripheral Interface) was developed by Motorola and contained four channels/wires:

   - **The SCLK:** refers to the master-driven serial clock

   - **The MOSI:** refers to the output by the master (which is the input to the slave)

   - **MISO:** it refers to the output by the master (which is the input to the slave)

   - **SS:** it refers to the slave-selection part of the wire.

And with that, we're over with your preliminary look into serial communication and its commonly used protocols. However, we're not ending the topic just yet. Since we're already on the topic of communication and signals, why not discuss one more much-needed distinction before we move on to the next chapter?

The Difference between Digital and Analog Signals

Ever since the start of the book, you might have read multiple references and mentions of digital and analog signals- don't worry, we won't let you go before satisfying your curiosity.

A digital signal is one that only has two states which are distinctly different in nature. For example, you could think of a lightbulb as a digital signal; in such an instance, switching a light on would be one state, whereas switching a light off would be another. These two states cannot overlap and take place distinctly; that is, they cannot both occur simultaneously, just like how you cannot turn a light on while keeping it off.

On the other hand, analog signals point to an infinite number of values. However, these values aren't infinite without a beginning or an end; rather, they point towards an infinite number of possible values between an already specified maximum and minimum value range. To present you with an analogy, you can think of sunlight; sunlight hits its maximum during the day and its minimum during the night. However, during the day, there are an almost infinite number of slight variations in the amount of sunlight you get exposed to as the sun goes from its maximum to minimum position and vice versa.

When working with microcontrollers or computers, digital signals are represented in Boolean (in case you didn't know, Boolean refers to 0 or 1 in computer terminology). The 0 here refers to the off state or the state where the light is switched off, whereas the 1 refers to the on state or the state in which the light is switched on. When it comes to digital signals in Arduino, you get a bit more convenient approach as the Boolean 0 and 1 are replaced by two set constants, namely HIGH and LOW.

On the other hand, Analog signals are pretty straightforward; they can be referred to as a real number or a floating number (refers to numbers in decimals, for example, 0.1, 0.3, etc.); there really isn't a restriction.

Chapter 11

Advanced Arduino Tricks

With that, you've discovered most of what this book has to offer. In the final chapter of this book, we'd like to offer you some tips and tricks of the trade which will not only benefit you in your beginning stages but will also continue to assist you as you continue to progress throughout your career.

What Are Some Advanced Arduino Techniques?

Freeing up Some RAM for Yourself

You should only opt for this technique if your project requires a lot of memory and you're stuck in a pinch. By using this method, you'll be able to you will be able to secure yourself at least 100 more bytes of RAM. If you're scoffing at it, you should remember what size the RAMs of Arduino boards normally are. You should also remember that 100 more bytes of RAM equal around 10% of the total RAM allocated to the ATmega168 microcontroller (considered quite a powerhouse when it comes to Arduino boards).

Now that the significance of 100 more bytes of space is out of the way, let's get into the meat and potatoes. You can create more space in your RAM by lessening the number of bytes allocated to the serial receive buffer; how can you go around doing this?

Well, for starters, you can start by opening up the hardware folder inside the Arduino setup files. Inside the Hardware directory is a subdirectory named cores, which contains another subdirectory named Arduino. Inside the Arduino subdirectory, you'll have to search for a file named HardwareSerial.cpp or wiring_serial.c; by default, Arduino allocated around 128 bytes of storage to the serial receive buffer, which is quite a lot and, frankly, unnecessary!

After you have located either of the two files, look towards the top and locate a line of code that will state the following:

#define RX_BUFFER_SIZE 128

You can change this line's "128" value to whatever you like! You can set it to 64, 32, 16, or even 1 as long as your program has no serial input. You can go as low as you want with the serial receive buffer as long as you fulfill the condition, that is, your program must have no serial input and the value you set must at least be great than 0.

Now, if you're really stingy, you can also save another 2 bytes of RAM by changing the following two lines of code:

int rx_buffer_head....

int rx_buffer_tail....

Within the same file to:

uint8_t rx_buffer_head....

uint8_t rx_buffer_tail....

Writing Proper Documentation

We have stressed a lot about proper documentation in this book. With how important proper documentation is looked upon in a professional setting and in large-scale companies, we believe it is only natural to end the final chapter of the book by once again revising the proper documentation techniques, which include:

- Opting for the proper naming conventions whenever you declare a variable, a function, an object, etc.

- Proper commenting; you don't really have to tell what the code is doing; just specifying the purpose of the code should be enough.

- Write additional materials related to your code, including anything from how you believe the code can be made more efficient to your ideas on how to proceed further with the code. Place this code within another header file (**Reminder:** Header files have a ".h" extension) meant solely for comments, not code.

Conclusion

Congratulations on making it this far! With this, we have reached the end of the book. Since you've reached this far, you've probably gone through all the concepts the book offers, and we're sure you're much more comfortable with Arduino than when you began reading the book.

At the end of this journey, we'd like to congratulate you on being so focused and committed to your goal, and most of all, we'd like to thank you for your interest in Arduino and, more importantly, for your interest in *Tips and Tricks for the Efficient Use of Arduino Programming.*

Finally, we'd like to sign off by saying that you shouldn't think a lot; at this stage of your career, you are allowed to make lots of mistakes, learn and grow. You should never make the fear of failure stop you from striving hard; rather, you should turn it into your motivation and learn along your journey, and with that last piece of advice, we're signing off. We wish you luck in your future endeavors!

Thank you for buying and reading/listening to our book. If you found this book useful/helpful please take a few minutes and leave a review on Amazon.com or Audible.com (if you bought the audio version).

References

2022, S. W. A. (2020). *Arduino Functions | How To Program and Use a Function*. Starting Electronics. https://startingelectronics.org/software/arduino/learn-to-program-course/15-functions/

A. (2021, January 23). *Scope Rules in C*. StudyMite. https://www.studymite.com/c-programming-language/scope-rules-in-c/

About. (2021, September 15). Arduino. https://www.arduino.cc/en/about/

Ada, L. A. (2013, January 12). *Arduino Tips, Tricks, and Techniques*. Adafruit Learning System. https://learn.adafruit.com/arduino-tips-tricks-and-techniques/

About. (2021, October 15). Arduino. https://www.arduino.cc/en/about/

Arduino Board Serial. (2022, July 7). Arduino Documentation. https://docs.arduino.cc/retired/boards/arduino-serial

All About Arduino Libraries. (2013, February 16). Adafruit Learning System. https://learn.adafruit.com/adafruit-all-about-arduino-libraries-install-use/arduino-libraries

Arduino Library List. (2022). Arduino Libraries. https://www.arduinolibraries.info/

Arthur, J. (2020). *Arduino: The complete guide to Arduino for beginners, including projects, tips, tricks, and programming!* [E-book]. Ingram Publishing.

Arduino - Strings. (2020). TutorialsPoint. https://www.tutorialspoint.com/arduino/arduino_strings.htm#:%7E:text=Strings%20are%20used%20to%20store,keypad%20connected%20to%20the%20Arduino.

Arduino String - JavaTpoint. (2020). JavaTpoint. https://www.javatpoint.com/arduino-string#:%7E:text=The%20string%20is%20a%20data,characters%20from%20the%20ASCII%20table.

Arduino Tips, Tricks and Techniques https://cdn-learn.adafruit.com/downloads/pdf/arduino-tips-tricks-and-techniques.pdf *(2022)*

array - Arduino Reference. (2021, October 20). Arduino. https://www.arduino.cc/reference/en/language/variables/data-types/array/

Azzola, F. (2018, August 27). *10 Arduino IDE alternative to start programming*. Java Code Geeks. https://www.javacodegeeks.com/2018/08/10-arduino-ide-alternative.html

Bayle, J. (2013). *C Programming for Arduino*. Packt Publishing.

Boloor, A. J. (2015). *Arduino by Example*. Van Haren Publishing.

Gupta, P. (2021, March 4). *Types of Arduino*. EDUCBA. https://www.educba.com/types-of-arduino/

Instructables. (2019, June 30). *Smarter Arduino Programming - Tips and Tricks*. https://www.instructables.com/Smarter-Arduino-Programming-Tips-and-Tricks/

JIMBLOM. (2022). *Efficient Arduino Programming with Arduino CLI and Visual Studio Code - learn.sparkfun.com*. Sparkfun. https://learn.sparkfun.com/tutorials/efficient-arduino-programming-with-arduino-cli-and-visual-studio-code/all

M. (2020, September 27). *5 tips for Arduino programs*. MegunoLink. https://www.megunolink.com/articles/5-tips-for-arduino-programs/

Nussey, J. (2018). *Arduino For Dummies (For Dummies (Computer/Tech))* (2nd ed.) [E-book]. For Dummies.

Perea, F. (2015). *Arduino Essentials* (Illustrated ed.) [E-book]. Packt Publishing.

R. (2015, May 21). *Assigning one array to another*. Arduino Forum. https://forum.arduino.cc/t/assigning-one-array-to-another/312875

Software. (2022). Arduino. https://www.arduino.cc/en/software/

Thorpe, E. (2020). *Arduino: Advanced Methods and Strategies of Using Arduino* [E-book]. Independently published.

Using Functions in a Sketch. (2022, July 7). Arduino Documentation. https://docs.arduino.cc/learn/programming/functions

W. (2015, April 30). *Arduino Tips & Tricks*. CodeProject. https://www.codeproject.com/Tips/987180/Arduino-Tips-Tricks

Wirz, M. W. (2022, March 22). *Types of Arduino Boards – Quick Comparison on Specification and Features.* CircuitDigest. https://circuitdigest.com/article/different-types-of-arduino-boards

Yadav, R. D. (2021, December 14). *Create Your Own Arduino Library (.h and .cpp files).* Medium. https://rishabhdevyadav.medium.com/create-your-own-arduino-library-h-and-cpp-files-62ab456453e0

Zahid, B. H. (2022, February). *Serial Communication in Arduino.* LinuxHint. https://linuxhint.com/serial-communication-in-arduino/#:%7E:text=In%20Arduino%2C%20%E2%80%9C Serial%20Communication%E2%80%9D,are%20dedicated %20for%20this%20purpose.